ONE HUNDRED Fascinating LOUISVILLE WOMEN

Nancy Miller

Photography by John Nation

Design by Hill Harcourt

CRESCENT HILL BOOKS

100 Fascinating Louisville Women

Published by

Crescent Hill Books

2410 Frankfort Avenue

Louisville, KY 40206

1-800-401-6838

www.crescenthillbooks.com

ISBN 978-1-889937-14-4

Printed in China through Four Color Imports Print Group, Louisville, Kentucky

Cover and book design by

Hill Harcourt, President, Ashton Advertising, Louisville, Kentucky

www.ashtonadvertising.com

Acknowledgments

Interviewing and getting to know the women in this book was an experience to treasure.
I thank them all.

Many people agreed that the idea for *100 Fascinating Louisville Women* had merit.
But, if it had not been for Hill Harcourt and Nancye Buckner, it would have been an idea
that languished. Thank you both for helping to make it a reality.

John Nation, your name should glow in the dark on the cover. Your photographs are stunning
illustrations of the women's spirits and personalities. Finally having the book in print is
bittersweet. Everyone can enjoy your work, but I miss working with you.

Hill, thank you for your creativity that unfolds from page to page. Your wit and singular
perspective are, themselves, subjects for a sure-fire hit of a book.

Nancy Heinonen and George Dick of Crescent Hill Books, I'm so grateful that you had faith in
the book and were enthusiastic about publishing it. And thank you for guiding us through the
process and masterminding the production.

Sometimes we neglect to thank the people who mean the most to us. Vicki Schmidt, Lisa
Strother, Kathy McHugh, and Susan Crook, thank you for being fascinating, wonderful friends.
Donna Pence, you are fun and funny, unpredictable, wicked, gracious and loving. I don't know
what I did to deserve you for a friend, nor do I know what I would do without your friendship.

Alex, you often questioned whether this book would ever be finished. Well, here it is.
Told you so! It is to you I owe the most thanks. You make me happy and proud.
And thank you for still letting me call you Sweet Pea.

I would have loved to have been able to include my mother in this book. She was strong and
courageous and independent. She was truly fascinating. It has taken me awhile to realize that
she was the inspiration for the book.

Nancy Miller

fas·ci·nat·ing

[fas-uh-ney-ting]

adjective

of great interest or attraction; enchanting; charming; captivating

Contents

Emily Albrink

As a soprano, you've performed with the Kentucky Opera, Washington National Opera, Baltimore Symphony, the Philharmonic Orchestra and the Chicago Opera, to name a few. How did it all begin?

I have had a career on the stage in some capacity since I can remember. At age 11, while we were living in Omaha, I performed my first solo, with the Omaha Symphony. After returning to Louisville, while at Walden Theatre —a one-of-a-kind theatre company—I discovered I loved acting as much as singing. I went to the University of Michigan thinking I wanted to do musical theatre. It wasn't what I thought it would be, but having that background of understanding the importance of words and communicating now sets me apart. I sing a lot of new music from living composers, mostly Americans who write in English. I think they like me because I can express their work in a beautiful, natural way. I enjoy working with living composers on their new material because I can talk to them and ask, "What was your intent? How do you want this to sound?"

How do you get your roles?

Most opera companies hold auditions for three weeks every November and December. I audition for as many companies as possible for their upcoming seasons.

Your career is full of remarkable successes, but there must have been some disappointments. How do you deal with those?

Everyone has "off days." I can definitely tell when an audition didn't go well. Other times I have thought I was great but didn't get the role. That's just part of the business and I have to accept it. When you get to my level, everyone is talented. It's expected that we have mastered our technique; our intonation and diction must be perfect. Opera also involves acting well and looking good. I'm a light lyric soprano, the most common type. Any given success depends on bringing something special and different to the role.

But you stress that there's much more to being an opera singer than singing.

I practice every day but I'm also constantly marketing myself. Frankly, the business is 10 percent talent, 40 percent connections and 50 percent hard work.

What has been your favorite role?

Susanna, the maid in The Marriage of Figaro, at The Kennedy Center. She's onstage all the time. She masterminds everything that goes on, and she is honest, clever, and funny.

You've already had many memorable moments in your career. Which ones particularly stand out?

My first Mozart role was also my first role in Italian, and it was my first starring role in a full-length opera. It was in Cosi fan tutte, performed at the Tanglewood Music Festival, and conducted by the renowned James Levine. It was an unbelievable, life-changing experience. Of course I was completely honored. He told me I needed to sing everything as if it were in my native language. I learned that if you're true to the word, the rest will follow. Storytelling—that's the reason I also loved theatre. When I'm singing, I want to communicate to the audience, make them change their minds or move them in some way. I want an emotional connection to the text, an expressivity and real honesty.

I also had the amazing opportunity to work with Dawn Upshaw, one of the most famous American sopranos, at Tanglewood. Later, I made my main stage Carnegie Hall debut with her. I couldn't believe I was actually standing on the stage with her. Just after I had begun singing during rehearsal, she said, "I'm so glad I was here when you sang your first line at Carnegie Hall." That was truly a wonderful moment for me. She is a very humble, warm, and open person who has been so helpful to me in getting gigs. I want to have that spirit and to be able to pass along the torch.

Do you consider yourself a diva?

I hope I'm never thought of as a diva because the word has such a negative connotation. The composer and the music should always come first. I'm only a vessel. I don't want my ego to ever get in the way of that.

With what person of note would you most like to spend the day?

Oprah.

What's the best decision you've made?

To carve out my own path and not feel as if I needed to conform to the musical theatre or to the opera world.

It might be impossible to imagine, but what would you want to do if you weren't an opera singer?

I'd like to be in fashion. Or maybe be an interior designer.

Elmer Lucille Allen

It might come as a surprise to some people that you had a much different career long before you became an artist.
I was a chemist at American Synthetic Rubber and at the University of Louisville. I was the first African-American chemist at Brown-Forman and one of only three women employed at the company in 1966. Prior to working as a chemist, I was a medical technician.

You're very gracious and open about sharing your experiences as a young African-American in Louisville.
When I graduated high school in 1949, Louisville was segregated. I attended Louisville Municipal College, which was an all-black college established by the University of Louisville. Later I attended Nazareth College, which became Spalding University. While I was in college there were many restaurants that refused to serve African-Americans. In fact, we weren't able to have a graduation party where we wanted because there were two African-Americans in our class.

At first I felt like an outsider at Brown-Forman. There were no professional blacks in the company. Blacks were only maids, janitors, and cooks. I had to be social, but I had to let everyone know I had been hired to do my job. Being in a mostly all-white organization was difficult and I constantly had to be on the offensive. I couldn't let anyone walk over me; I had to stand my ground, prove myself, and be strong. I was there 31 years. There have always been obstacles for me as an African-American, but I've found avenues to pursue. It's still a battle for African-Americans. We have to be better than our counterparts to get the same respect, but I'm not negative about it.

You're a widely recognized fiber artist and ceramicist. Your life as an artist came relatively late in life.
I started to work with ceramics when I took an adult education course at Seneca High School. I had arthritis and it was a way to use my hands. I received my master's degree in creative arts from the University of Louisville when I was 71 years old. I love working with clay. I'm fascinated by the thinking process involved. I especially enjoy making teapots. I may do a series of them, but each one is different. I sketch them out before I begin and think about the kind of clay I want to use and how I want to texture it. Each piece changes as I create it. Not every piece is a good one. I might make ten but only really like one. I'm also doing a lot of shibori, a Japanese technique of dyeing, binding, stitching, folding, and twisting fabric.

Even though you're well established in the art community, have received numerous awards, are the director and curator of Wayside Christian Mission's art gallery, and are a mentor to other artists, you say your education isn't over.
I'm a perpetual student and still take classes. I enjoy young people and the artistic environment.

What do you like best about yourself?
I was brought up to love, to share, and to give.

What do you want from other people?
I want them to be positive and truthful.

Are you technologically savvy?
I want to be part of the digital highway because it's the future. I like to be seen and heard, but I don't text and I'm not on Twitter or Facebook. They take too much time.

What haven't you done that you'd like to do?
I'd like to travel, especially to Africa. But with the way the world is now, I'll stay in the United States where it's safer.

What woman has had the most profound effect on you?
I accomplished many things on my own, but my mother set the example for me. She was a day worker, working in people's kitchens, ironing their clothes, doing whatever they wanted or needed. From her I learned how to work and to do the best job I could do.

How do you feel about aging?
It doesn't bother me because it's part of life. I have struggled and have overcome a lot. I wouldn't mind experiencing some of the good things again, but I wouldn't want to relive my life. I certainly wouldn't want to be 16 again. I'm always looking ahead to what I can do or where I can go next.

Jayshree Amin

Your life growing up in India was one of wealth and privilege, but you were not removed from the harsh realities of the lives of other people.
Although we had servants and I never had to do anything for myself, even pour a glass of milk, I knew there were many people who were suffering. From the time I was very young, our family adopted several orphans and paid for their housing, food, and education. My husband and I continue to do that, and every year my grown son and daughter donate their January paychecks to a mission.

Was coming to the United States a major adjustment?
The most profound adjustment was seeing how independent people were, especially women, in the United States. At the time I left India, there were many social pressures on women. But here, the sky is the limit if you set goals. I won't lie and say I didn't miss having servants. Before I moved to America, I had asked our cook to teach me some of his favorite recipes. He gave me the wrong recipes because he didn't want me to be successful with them, hoping I would bring him here to cook for us. I soon realized I enjoyed cooking, but doing the dishes and cleaning up were new experiences for me.

How have you maintained your religious and cultural heritages?
My husband and I donated the land for and we are the largest sponsors of the Hindu temple in Louisville. And we have a temple in our house. We pray there every morning. Also, for 20 years we have funded Pujya Swamigi Chandandki's development of the first Hindu encyclopedia.

What were your aspirations when you were young?
I studied to be an architect and wanted to pursue that career. When I came to Louisville I worked for an architectural firm. I would still like to practice architecture. Of course, coming to the United States was always a fantasy of mine. That fantasy came true.

Were you opposed to an arranged marriage?
Not at all. I knew that my parents would introduce me to a boy who came from a good family and who had good morals and character. I didn't have to worry about screening him. But if it didn't click, there would be no pressure for me to marry the person. I fell in love with the man who was to become my husband the minute I met him. He felt the same way about me.

You are one of the best-dressed women in Louisville. Your passion for clothes and shopping often takes you to fashion capitals of the world, such as Paris. And your closet has to be seen to be believed!
I love clothes. My dad spoiled me. He wanted to be sure we presented well. My husband is the same way.

What would people be surprised to know about you?
That I'm a very simple person at heart. I could live in one bedroom and have a small kitchen and be as happy as I am today. They might also be surprised to know that I never take things for granted.

You run three medical practices that you and your husband own. But you still have time to host legendary parties. What makes them so spectacular?
I love to be around people, whether I'm having a small dinner party or an event for four hundred people in my home. Entertaining is my way of showing my friends how much I love them. I never forget the small details because they can be wonderful expressions of loving and caring. Also, I do all of my own cooking.

What are the most important lessons you have learned?
To work hard to achieve my goals. And to be generous.

Education and travel have played such important roles in your family's life.
Yes, we have always stressed the importance of education to our children. And we think it is imperative that they have a global perspective. Every year we take our children to a different continent.

In a few words, how would you describe yourself?
Passionate. Hardworking. Sensitive. And I like to enjoy life to the fullest.

What makes you angry?
I don't get angry unless someone really gets on my wrong side. I get upset if people hurt me although I have counted on them emotionally and would give up anything for them.

What would you change about your life if you could?
I would spend more time doing things for myself rather than being involved in so many activities. I'd love to sit on the deck overlooking the lake and read a book, but something else always comes up.

Ann Stewart Anderson

You're a painter and mosaic artist who concentrates on art about women. Do you find women more interesting than men?

Not necessarily. Some people aren't interesting at all and others are incredibly interesting. I'm not sure gender matters that much. Also, certain people are interesting to some people and not to others.

Why does your art focus on women?

I made that conscious decision in the mid '70s because women's issues were beginning to surface. I started thinking about the things women do for which we are made fun of or criticized. I wanted to honor women through those subjects.

Your subjects range from women in Greek mythology to modern women putting on their makeup. There don't seem to be any boundaries for you.

No, there aren't. I like to depict the roles women play in their daily lives, regardless of when they live. One of the first works was The Vanity Series. Funny and poignant, they grew out of a Mary Kay Cosmetics party. I didn't want to go to the party because you're told if you do this and that you'll be instantly beautiful. But it led me to paint multiple panels of women sitting at their vanities looking in the mirrors. One of the women is wistfully looking in the mirror, obviously worried that it won't work out quite the way Mary Kay told us. After that I painted Women Having Hot Flashes, something with which many of us can identify.

When I started observing women in ladies' rooms, I was tickled to see that women are so mesmerized by putting on their makeup that they don't look at each other. Most of the time when women meet they say, "Oh, what a nice dress" or "Where did you get your shoes?" But they don't say anything to each other in the ladies' room. So I decided to do a series of groups of women putting on their makeup in public ladies' rooms.

I also did a series of women in conversation because I'm interested in how women sit around and gossip, in person or on the phone. The way most women find out the things that are really important to us is if another woman tells us.

You seem to take a humorous approach to women's attempt to beautify themselves or change their appearance.

While the message to be more beautiful is always there, now the emphasis seems to be on filling in the wrinkles or not getting them in the first place.

There's some new spackling every time we turn around, promising that in six weeks we'll look four years younger. I love cosmetics and I've surrendered. You think my face looks old now, but you should see what it would look like if I didn't do anything to it.

Humor isn't the entire story of your feelings about women's desire to make themselves more attractive.

No, the story is a bit more complicated. I had a glamorous aunt who was always put together and had nice jewelry. She developed lung cancer. When I asked her what I could bring her in the hospital, she told me there was a new perfume she'd like. And she was still very concerned about her appearance. But a week or two before she died, she stopped wearing makeup. I think that's interesting and an important insight. She was saying she was ready to die, that she no longer wanted blush and lipstick to look healthy.

Why has Greek mythology captured your imagination and become the inspiration for much of your work?

For the past decade I have concentrated on women's stories from Greek mythology—the sagas of Demeter and Persephone, Medea, Penelope, and Arachne. Mythic in stature, these figures embody the essential attributes of all women; showing these women's histories explains our own. Telling their stories visually enables me to discover the archetypal sister, mother, daughter, and wife. These paintings are essential statements about the vicissitudes of human life.

Do you think you've "found" yourself?

It's a continual journey. Maybe when you find yourself you're ready to go onto the next life.

What do you least like about yourself?

I get cross and moody. To get out of a bad mood, I leave the situation or "take myself to the woodshed" and say, "Look at life." How I get out of the mood depends on what put me in it in the first place.

What haven't you done that you'd like to do?

I'd love to do archeology. If I had nine lives, that would be one of them. I like to research and dig around and hunt things.

Catherine Todd
Bailey

President George Bush had quite a surprise for you.
I was to introduce him before a crowd of fourteen hundred people at an event in Louisville. I had been rehearsing my introduction for months. He was the leader of the free world! Just prior to my introduction and his speech, he looked at me and said, "By the way, it would mean a great deal to me if you would serve the United States abroad. I'd like to talk to you about it further." I was extremely honored and taken aback. I think I may have crinkled my notes.

I was asked to be the U.S. Ambassador to Latvia. Within two weeks I was at the White House and went through a vetting process. I had to appear before the Senate Foreign Relations Committee and was confirmed by the U.S. Senate.

Serving as an ambassador must be as exciting as it is challenging.
It exceeded my expectations. To be asked to serve the president and my country was such an honor. We were just coming off 9/11 and President Bush was focusing on the global war on terrorism. Formerly part of the Soviet Union, Latvia had been through so many atrocities. They understood the threat of terrorism all too well. It was an extraordinary experience to watch the relations between the two countries be nurtured and developed. In addition to executing the policies on behalf of the U.S., I wanted to share our culture whenever possible. We had art from Kentucky put in the residence and featured a quilt from Bardstown in the embassy. The Latvian people are just wonderful. I tried to interact with them whenever I had the opportunity. I was so proud to see how the United States helps elevate a country. It was phenomenal to watch U.S. soldiers and the Latvian soldiers working side by side with such precision and expertise at the NATO Summit in Riga, Latvia. It was one of the most overwhelming experiences of my life. We pulled it off with grace and ease.

You experienced a personal tragedy that few people could imagine.
Our two grandchildren were killed in a fire at our house on Christmas morning. There was a level of total desperation to save the boys. You don't come through that without knowing what you're made of. You can bury yourself and not come up for air or you can rally around each other and pull yourselves up. It made our family stronger. We will move forward and find a way to make something positive out of something so devastating.

My parents gave me a Bible when I was baptized at the age of 13. I was sworn in to the State Department by Colin Powell on my great-great-grandfather's Bible. That was the Bible I took with me to Latvia. Because of their age, I had stored the Bibles in separate zip-sealed plastic. A few months following the fire, I was sorting through the rubble. I froze as I looked down and saw my great-great-grandfather's Bible. Some pages were destroyed but overall it was intact. I walked a few more steps and found the bag with the Bible I received at my baptism. Finding those reminded me that I had influences around me that were helping me remain strong for my family.

Why did you found Operation Open Arms, an organization that provides care for babies while their mothers are incarcerated?
Throughout the country there are about five hundred thousand children who have a parent behind bars. If a child is put in a loving environment, he or she will have a better life and will have a better chance of becoming a responsible citizen. Operation Open Arms started with one family and we're now up to 13 families. I want to take the organization into every state because every child deserves a chance.

Other than the people in your life, what couldn't you live without?
We lost everything the day of the fire. Because we lost the boys, nothing else matters. If I didn't have my moral compass, the foundation that makes me kick, I would be a lost soul.

Would you ever consider running for office?
As soon as I say I'm not going to do something, another window opens. I think Kentucky has been held back by the people who have been leading it. I love Kentucky and want to be able to give back. If I see an opportunity that I can bring leadership to, I would probably say yes.

Susan Bandy

You funded your college education by dressing up as a bee?

I was the mascot for Burger Queen, a chain of fast-food restaurants based in Louisville. It was a very cool thing. I was in television commercials, made personal appearances, and wrote the company training manual.

Later you went to New York to seek your fame and fortune.

I wanted to be a Broadway star. I moved to New York and started taking an acting course. I was lucky to be selected to be in Woody Allen's *Broadway Danny Rose*. Unfortunately, all of my scenes were cut. I was also in *Desperately Seeking Susan*, which starred Madonna. If you're really good with the remote you can freeze the frame and catch me.

Why did you come back to Louisville?

To be with my father, who had had a massive stroke.

It was then that your long and very special relationship with McDonald's began.

When my father was released from the hospital he wasn't even able to move and had to go to rehab. But he had no health insurance. He had been Ronald McDonald since I was a teenager. I called the head of the McDonald's Louisville co-op and said I needed $5,000 to get him into rehab. He eventually incurred $200,000 in medical bills. The local McDonald's operators paid every penny.

While he was going back and forth between rehab and nursing homes, I got a job as account coordinator at Bon Advertising. One of the agency's accounts was McDonald's. I was asked to go to Chicago for the Ronald McDonald convention. When I walked in, I was shocked to see a sign with a get-well message to my father. The sign was strictly in his honor. No one there knew I was coming. It was something that was meant to be.

You started as account coordinator and bought the agency three years later. That was a fast track!

I realized I was very good in the business, and I loved it. I used to say I would never have a permanent job because I couldn't imagine doing the same thing every day. But it's never the same from one day to the next. Our agency, now Bandy Carroll Hellige, is very high-energy. The work is creative and diverse. And we work with McDonald's. What's not to love?

How did you decide to take to the air?

I was always on the road working, trying to get everywhere I needed to be and still be able to spend a lot of time at home with my son. Many places I go aren't served by commercial airlines. About the time I was wondering what it would cost to rent a plane, I decided I'd take a discovery flight for the heck of it. I soloed a month later. I bought a plane—not the smartest thing I've ever done. Planes are a great deal of work and are expensive. Flying back to Louisville from a business trip, I lost a cylinder. I wasn't at all panicked. When I landed at Bowman Field I discovered that the plane had a major problem and that I was lucky to have successfully landed. It took major work to restore the plane. I took away the big message that I wasn't supposed to own a plane anymore, and I sold it.

What haven't you done that you would like to do?

I used to say "jump out of a plane" but I don't think I want to do that anymore. I'd like to go to the Super Bowl, and I want to travel, but in my own way. I like adventure, and I prefer to stay in small hotels off the beaten path, not luxury hotels.

What do you like best about yourself?

I'm extremely positive. Some people might call it Pollyanna-ish. Also, I listen very hard to my intuition and am not afraid to act on that. Time and time again my gut instinct has been right on.

What traits do you most like in a person?

Humor and honesty. I like people who are forthright and direct but not rude or brutal. The whole environment of political correctness drives me crazy.

In your opinion, who's the most fascinating woman in history?

Joan of Arc. I have been to many of the places she had been. I've even been to where she was burned at the stake and where her ashes are buried.

Robbie Bartlett

You were a child prodigy!

I don't know about that, but I started singing in churches when I was four years old. I loved it then and I love it now.

People often say that you have such style, meaning your demeanor, attitude, and music. So, how would you describe your style of music?

Style? It's more like styles. I sing rhythm and blues, blues, jazz, and rock, but my favorite is jazz.

And the music comes from your soul.

Oh, yes. I sing from my soul. Otherwise I wouldn't do it. If I don't mean it, I won't sing it. I don't think I'm a great writer, but I write a little music. I recently did my first sound track for a movie. That was fun.

You opened for Frank Sinatra at the Louisville Palace. That must have been quite an experience.

It was wonderful. But I didn't get to meet him. They put him in the big dressing room. It's hard to meet the headliners even if you're opening for them.

You have performed during three tours in Europe and you're a fixture in many restaurants and clubs in Louisville. But there's still part of you that many people don't know.

I can be a loner. I'm a bit shy but people don't believe it. I can turn on my personality in public, but that's the entertaining side of me. And that's how I release my feelings. I'm genuinely happy that people come to see and hear me. I love people.

Do you sing to one person or the entire room?

Most of the time I close my eyes and just feel the song. My mother always said, if you don't feel it, don't expect your audience to feel it. I put on a show, but I'm actually feeling it. I don't want to be in the category of just acting. I'm not a very good actor. I'm nervous before I sing. I'm scared to get over that because you want to stay humble and hungry.

What's been the most significant accomplishment in your life?

To be able to do the job I absolutely love and have it actually pay the bills.

It must be hard to imagine yourself as anything but a singer. But what would you do if you weren't a singer?

Probably own a bed and breakfast somewhere in the mountains.

What's the biggest risk you've ever taken?

Singing with strep throat. I didn't know if the notes would even come out. What a horrible feeling. Luckily, they did come out. I didn't want to cancel the gig because I'd be putting my band out of work.

Your life may soon undergo a major change!

That's so right. I'm adopting a child from Guatemala. The process has taken a few years and is ongoing and very frustrating. I picked him out when he was two months old and saw him for the first time when he was four months old. Since then I have seen him many times. He calls me Mommy. I'm so ready to be a mother. I have his room all ready.

You have said it's your way or the highway.

Being a female band leader is harder than being a male band leader. Some of the older guys would try to run me. I have told them that if they want to run a band, put some players together and have a band. But in my band, we're going to do it my way.

Do you think it's more difficult to be a woman than a man, in general?

We have to do so much more to be noticed. We have to go overboard and that's not fair. Being a black woman is even harder.

You don't hide your feelings about wimpy people.

They irritate me. They don't have to be wimpy. It's a choice. I used to be passive, but that doesn't get you anywhere, and I want to go somewhere.

Many performers are known for their egos. What about you?

I don't have a big ego. People will ask a singer, "Are you good?" I always say I haven't been kicked out of anywhere. I just do what I do and hope people like it.

Is there anything people would be surprised to know about you?

I love anything John Deere. I have a John Deere lawn tractor. It was the closest I could get to a field tractor. I also have a John Deere mail box. The mailman calls me Mrs. Deere and calls my Labrador John Deere although the dog's name is Manny, named after Peyton Manning. I'm a football fan.

Angela Bartley

**You're a trumpeter and flight instructor. You have your own CD.
You're a salsa instructor. And you portray famous people.
You seem to be lots of people rolled into one person.**
I started playing the trumpet when I was growing up in Russell, Kentucky, an area that's underserved and is an industrial nightmare. I was awarded a music scholarship to the University of Louisville. It was the country girl going to the city. I think of the trumpet as a gift in my hands because it has taken me to incredible places, both literally and figuratively. Bugling at Churchill Downs was an interesting experience. I got to wear a great outfit and people cheered after I played. But wearing a wool suit and boots can get very hot. And my lips got tired. When you're a bugler at Churchill Downs, getting other jobs is easy. I play at conventions, weddings, lots of events. I like doing those because I'm a social person. And the pay and conditions are better than at the track! I also teach the trumpet to high school students, which is very neat.

I made a CD, *Sounds of Kentucky.* No one, myself included, thought it would sell, but it has sold more than 20,000 copies. Two of its tracks were in the movie, *Gonzo: The Life of Work of Hunter S. Thompson.* I'm excited because I will have a new CD that will encompass even more of the Kentucky story.

You're queen of the free ride!
I was working at UPS in the day when employees could get free rides. I traveled in the jump seat to six continents. I had books full of experiences from all over the world. I loved the culture, art, and history of Western Europe, but New Zealand was my favorite. It has every climate, and fjords, beaches, and mountains. It's paradise.

But you got tired of being a passenger.
I loved flying so much I took lessons and became a flight instructor.

You're a dancer. Will we see you on *Dancing with the Stars*?
No! I teach salsa, but it's street dancing, which is social dancing. *Dancing with the Stars* is more competitive, with flips and all that.

When you're not flying or bugling or dancing, you pretend you're someone else?
I portray historical figures, such as Mary Todd Lincoln and Rosie the Riveter, at schools, libraries, luncheons, and many other events. I actually wrote the Rosie the Riveter scripts I perform. Sometimes, at the events where there are

real Rosies, women who worked in war-related industries during World War II, the community or attendees will recognize and acknowledge them for who they were and for the contributions they made. They're now in their eighties. It's very moving.

What do you like best about yourself?
Either through my teaching or having them know me as a role model, I have a real knack for helping people be the best they can be. I'm a good role model to show that you can live the life you want as long as you figure out how to do it and make it work. I'm a performing artist, and I went into areas that not a lot of women had gone into, such as being a bugler and a flight instructor. I'm a little unconventional, but I'm not a starving artist and I enjoy a nice lifestyle.

And least?
I can get really emotional, but that's also how I get a lot of strength. I love it and hate it.

What traits do you most like in a person?
An open mind and a compassionate spirit. I like people who are welcoming to everyone.

And least?
Racists. And I can't stand people who take advantage of others. They should burn in a fiery, hot place.

With which people of note, living or dead, would you most like to spend a day?
It's a stellar list: Buddha, Jesus Christ, Muhammad, the Pope, Abraham Lincoln, and Mary Todd Lincoln. We'd have lunch and a philosophical discussion.

What haven't you done that you'd like to do?
I want to write a book. I can't tell you what it's about because it's a secret. I also want to do more performing and would like to add characters to my repertoire. I'm considering Queen Elizabeth and Amelia Earhart.

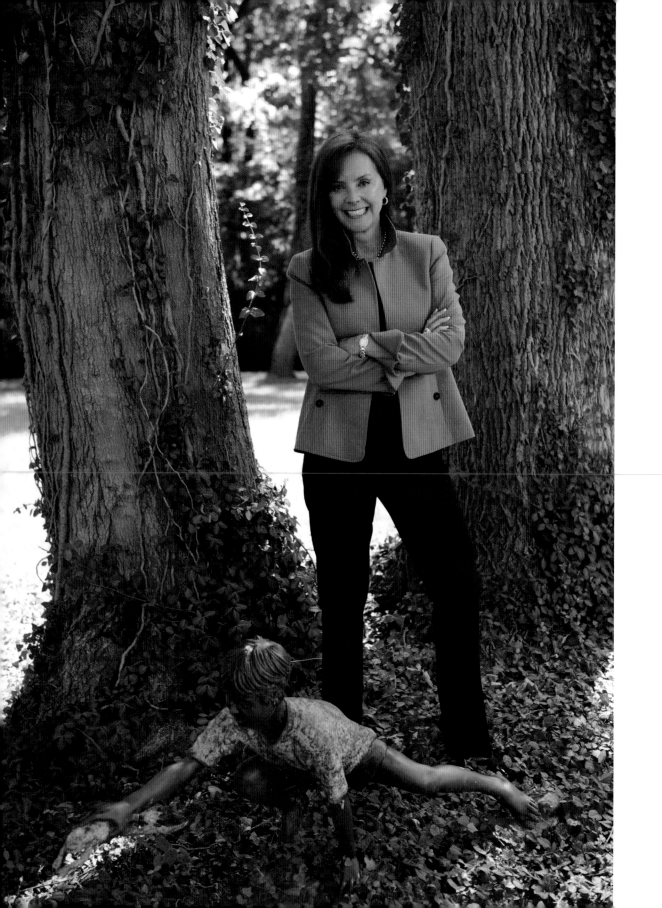

Terri Bass

You were instrumental in starting Court Appointed Special Advocates (CASA) in Louisville. What initiated your involvement with children's issues?

My awareness of children's issues, particularly child abuse, began when I was active with the Junior League and the National Council for Jewish Women. I was also a volunteer at Home of the Innocents and saw abused children who would return again and again. I was involved in a committee of the Junior League that focused on child abuse. I couldn't conceive how children could live in such horrible situations and why society would allow children to be put back into dangerous homes. The courts were overloaded, social workers had too many cases, and judges had to make decisions based on little information. Our research showed that CASA programs had been effective in other states. With the help of the National Council for Jewish Women and the Junior League, we brought CASA to Louisville.

CASA trains volunteers to be the eyes and ears of the court and to be mentors to the children as they go through the court system. CASA helps find relatives who may be able to care for the children, cutting down children's time in foster care. We also look into various factors that are impacting the children and their families. The success stories are amazing.

My husband and I renovated a historic home and opened it for events and fundraisers for organizations that are important to us, such as the Brown Cancer Center and Gilda's Club. It isn't important to me to have my name on a board list. I really focus my energy and time on children's needs. I'm happy to contribute to the arts organizations because I know they're very important and serve the community, but when it comes to giving my time, I usually focus on abused, abandoned, or neglected children.

What has been the major challenge in your life?

Mothering and being a good parent. We lost a little boy, Elliott, when he was ten days old. That was an amazing lesson. He taught me that every day is precious. I rely on the strength he gave me. Nothing is too daunting. I don't get blown away by the little things in life. Elliott was born on July 17. One year to the day later, my son Joel was diagnosed with cancer in his senior year of high school. I thought I couldn't handle any more. Fortunately, he was given a 75 percent chance of kicking it. Neither he nor I were going to be wimpy about fighting. We were successful. He is now 38 years old, healthy, married, and living a terrific life.

Is there anything that intimidates you?

Public speaking.

Have you ever done anything totally out of character?

I was asked to participate in the local *Dancing with the Stars* to benefit the Louisville Orchestra. The thought of performing in front of all those people just about did me in. I had a few missteps in the beginning, but I pulled it together and had fun. I even won the People's Choice Award.

What's the most important thing you've learned about yourself?

Years ago I measured myself, or compared myself, to people I thought were more accomplished or were doing a better job than I was doing, whatever that happened to be. I felt lacking. I'm my biggest critic. But in the past few years, with a conscious effort, I have begun to trust my own abilities and instincts to a much greater extent. I'm a happier person, a better wife and mother, and a more effective community volunteer because I don't worry about what other people think.

What haven't you done that you'd like to do?

Spend time in Africa and China.

How do you feel about aging?

I think we have a real age and another age in our mind's eye. I don't mind admitting my age. I'm 58, but in my mind's eye I'm 36. That changes every now and then, but I have been 34ish or 36ish for a number of years. I don't worry about aging too much. I try to do things that keep me healthy and focus on the fact that we have only today. If I can live the day well and do something for someone else, I feel it has been a good day.

What would people be surprised to know about you?

I was a lumber buyer and I know how to drive a forklift.

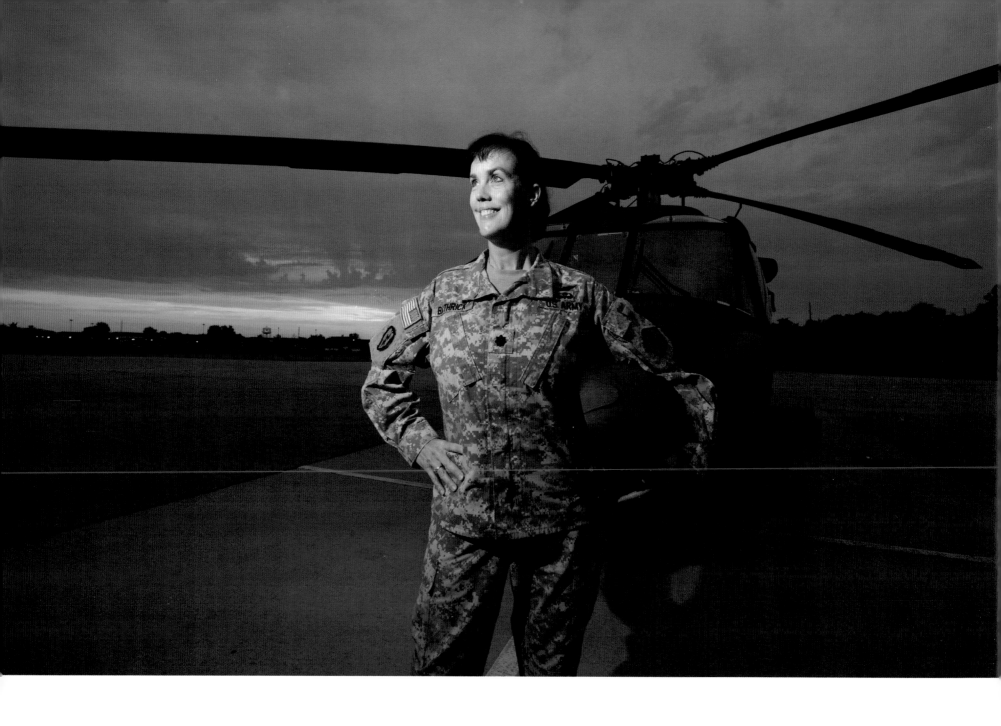

Stacy Bathrick

You're a lieutenant colonel in the U.S. Army. You are a Chinook helicopter pilot who served in Afghanistan, the Philippines, and South Korea. In Afghanistan you were part of combat patrols with embedded reporters from CBS, NBC, and FOX. And you interfaced with football Hall of Famer John Elway and actor Robin Williams. You're an extremely visible face of the U.S. Army!

I'm so proud to be able to help carry the Army's story to the public because I love serving our country. But I try to not be the visible one because the real heroes are the soldiers on the ground, the ones who are putting their lives on the line every day.

Even in the modern Army, for a woman to achieve the rank of lieutenant colonel is quite a distinction. What's the inside story of being a woman in the military?

You're always giving your personal best, being your own worst critic, and seeing the challenges around you as something that can make you stronger. Have I felt discrimination because I'm female? Not from my superiors, but I have experienced discrimination and intimidation from my peers. But I knew they could only make me feel inferior if I let them do that. I have always done everything I can to show them that their tactics aren't going to work because I'm going to perform better than they do and I'll come out ahead and get the last laugh. It hasn't been easy. But I don't use that as a crutch. I hope I have paved the way for other women, just as there were women who made the road easier for me to travel.

You completed the U.S. Army Aviation, Survival, Evasion, Resistance, and Escape training as well as the Electronic Warfare Officer Course. What's your response to people who say there are certain areas of the military from which women should be excluded?

I trust the decisions that get made by the senior leaders of the Army. They understand that the battlefield is much different today than in the past. There's now an Army pilot program that allows women in certain units, down to the battalion level, to be doing their specialties. When I took Geraldo Rivera to an Army camp along the Afghanistan/Pakistan border, the base started to get rocketed. I was the only female there and it didn't make one bit of difference. The instincts of all of us kicked in and we all did what we were trained to do.

Other than the people in your life, what couldn't you live without?

My values. They keep me grounded. I'm blessed to have a balance of family, God, and career. My emotions run deep because of the experiences I have had in the military. I never take a day for granted.

There must have been enough experiences in the Army for you to write a book.

When I was in Afghanistan, I thought I wanted to write a book. I journaled as key events happened. But what I really want to write about is how the Army has prepared me for motherhood, for what matters most in my life. Being a mother is the most important job I will ever have.

You have faced many formidable challenges. What one particularly stands out?

My husband was in Iraq for 15 months. I potty trained our twins by myself. I consider that quite an accomplishment!

Is there anything that intimidates you?

No. The military has done an awesome job preparing me for anything.

What would people be surprised to know about you?

That I'm a strong Christian. I really don't discuss it with folks. But I try to live my life the way I believe Jesus Christ wants me to live it.

How would you finish the sentence, "I wish women would. . .

always give their best in everything they do, realizing that sometimes they have to do more than men just to be considered good enough, and not get bitter or angry or hold any grudges while they're doing it." But that's okay.

Being a military officer in combat, you have gone to some of the most dangerous areas of the world, where most women, as well as men, will never go. You're a hero.

I don't feel that I'm a hero. I have been among soldiers who have paid the ultimate sacrifice. I chose a profession for which every day has been an absolute honor to serve. I've been able to be a part of a profession of arms, a band of brothers, a band of sisters. I have lived my dream. I feel like I'm the luckiest woman in the world.

Maria Kostandinithou Bell

Why were you eager to leave your hometown in Greece?

My two brothers and I were raised in a Greek Orthodox family in Ierapetra. It was a fishing village until the 1960s when it switched to agriculture. It was a small town where everyone knew everyone else's business. I hated that the townspeople were such gossips. I was a rebel and didn't stay a single day after high school. I moved to Athens and attended the university there for a couple of years until I decided to travel around Europe. When I returned to Athens I worked as a translator and also taught English. I had started learning English from tourists at the beach when I was seven years old. I also learned the language by using a pocket English dictionary. So it was natural for me to want to teach English to other people.

You fell in love and moved to the United States?

I met an American who was a disc jockey at the local radio station. One day he said on the air, "Good morning, my Maria." So many people listened to the station that I became the center of attention in town. It was exciting and flattering. We married and came to the United States. My first experience in America was in Washington, D.C. I couldn't believe how fast traffic was moving, not at all the way it was in Greece. I had seen only elephants and tigers in a circus in Greece and wanted to go to the zoo. I was thrilled to see the giraffes and so many animals I had never seen before. We moved to Tucson where I taught children from Greek families how to speak Greek so they would still have a tie to their culture. I became very unhappy. We returned to Greece where I gave birth to a daughter. My husband and I were such different people that the marriage just couldn't work, and we divorced.

You were a retailer for awhile.

I had a store named after my daughter, Vidie. We sold women's clothing and jewelry.

When you came to the United States the second time, you decided to make it home.

I met someone in the U.S. Air Force who was stationed in Greece. He convinced me to get married although I really didn't want to do that. We moved to Ft. Knox and eventually got divorced, but I liked Kentucky and stayed.

This is where your professional life in food began.

I learned to cook from my mother and grandmother. I cooked for friends and family but never thought of it as a profession. When we were stationed at Ft. Knox there weren't many dining options. I opened Greek Paradise Café, and people discovered they loved Greek food. When I opened my restaurant in Louisville, we added music and dancing. It was lively and lots of fun. I still love the chance to introduce people to Greek cuisine.

What do you most miss about your life in Greece?

The concept of the extended Greek family. No one ever called before they visited; they simply came over. The next thing I knew, we were eating and drinking and talking. That spontaneity doesn't happen here. Everyone wants to make plans before they go out or visit friends. I miss the knock on the door.

What's the best decision you ever made?

To stay single after my divorce.

And your biggest regret?

That I didn't have more than one child.

How would you describe yourself?

Vivacious and extroverted.

What do you like best about yourself?

I'm a hard worker. I'm amazed that I can have a long, difficult day, go to bed, and get up in the morning with a very positive attitude and great energy. I'm eager to start all over.

What's the most important thing you have learned about yourself?

I have discovered more about myself and appreciate myself more the older I get. I also accept people as they are and I am not as judgmental as I was earlier in my life. I've finally learned that I can't change them.

Other than the people in your life, what couldn't you live without?

My iPad.

What would you do if you weren't a chef?

Teach English in Latin America.

How do you feel about aging?

I'm ready.

Is there anything you'd like to change about yourself?

I'd like to be less naive.

What's next for you?

I want to go to Tibet. And I want to teach Greek cooking and slow food cooking.

Carol Besse

You and your husband founded what is now Louisville's oldest bookstore. What led you into the book business?

We worked for a small bookstore chain in Chicago before we decided to move to Louisville. Originally, we had considered moving to Lexington, but when W. K. Stewart's bookstore closed in 1978, we opened our store.

Carmichael's is recognized as one of the country's leading independent bookstores. How have you survived in a struggling industry?

I think there are three things that have contributed to our longevity. The first is our size. We never had aspirations to take over the world. We are small and are nestled in our community and neighborhoods. Michael and I are still on the floor selling books every day. Another reason for our success is that we have established partnerships in the community that allow us to appear bigger than we are. Also, we benefit from the Shop Local movement.

What's it like being in business with your husband and being around each other all day, every day?

I love it. We have the kind of relationship that works. After so many years, we let the bad stuff roll off our backs. Carmichael's is a complete family operation. Every woman in our family works in the stores.

Many nationally-acclaimed authors have been guests at your stores. There must have been some real prima donnas.

Most of the authors we have hosted have been very humble and genuine people. Writing is a solitary activity, but marketing your book is the complete opposite of that. So, it's hard to have those two personality types in one person. I don't know that I have a favorite author who has come to our stores, although Barbara Kingsolver would be at the top of the list. She's wonderful, and I love that she's from Kentucky.

How have people's reading habits changed in the last five or ten years?

Fortunately, our business has been growing, so we don't see the decline in reading. But, statistics show that people are reading less. I think that has to do with today's pace of life. It might be argued that the media and Internet have shortened attention spans. We're so used to receiving information in short shots that sitting down and reading for a period of time can be difficult for some people. On the other hand, being still, focusing, and reading is even more important because of all the chaos that's going on in the world.

We wouldn't dare ask you to name your favorite books, but we wouldn't mind if you divulged them on your own.

I don't read much nonfiction, but *Small is Beautiful: Economics as if People Mattered* has been an important book to me because its premise is that on which I have sort of based my business. It's all about localism and relationships, and expanding that into an economic scheme. *One Hundred Years of Solitude* was one of the first novels that really captured me. And *Little Bee* is one of the best books I have read in the last five years.

What has been the biggest challenge of your life?

Dealing with my mother having Alzheimer's disease.

Is there anything you haven't done that you would like to do?

I'm a big birder, something I came to about ten years ago. I'm not obsessive, but I do keep a list of birds I have seen and those I have not seen. There are still many I want to see.

What do you worry about?

The environment. That's kind of tied into being a birder. Nature is such a delicate balance. We don't understand the implications of how one change affects everything down the line.

What do you like best about yourself?

That I can let things go. I don't hang on to the bad stuff, either on a day-to-day basis or in a big-picture way.

And least?

I can be kind of brusque and fairly direct.

How do you feel about aging?

It's hell. I am in fairly good health so far and I don't feel old yet. I think the Baby Boomer generation is one that refuses to accept aging, and I'm probably part of that.

Do you have any advice to young women?

Women are getting more active at a younger age, and that's good. They're also postponing marriage and family, and I think that's also a good thing. Older mothers tend to be more understanding and committed.

How would you finish the sentence, "I wish women would…
run the world."

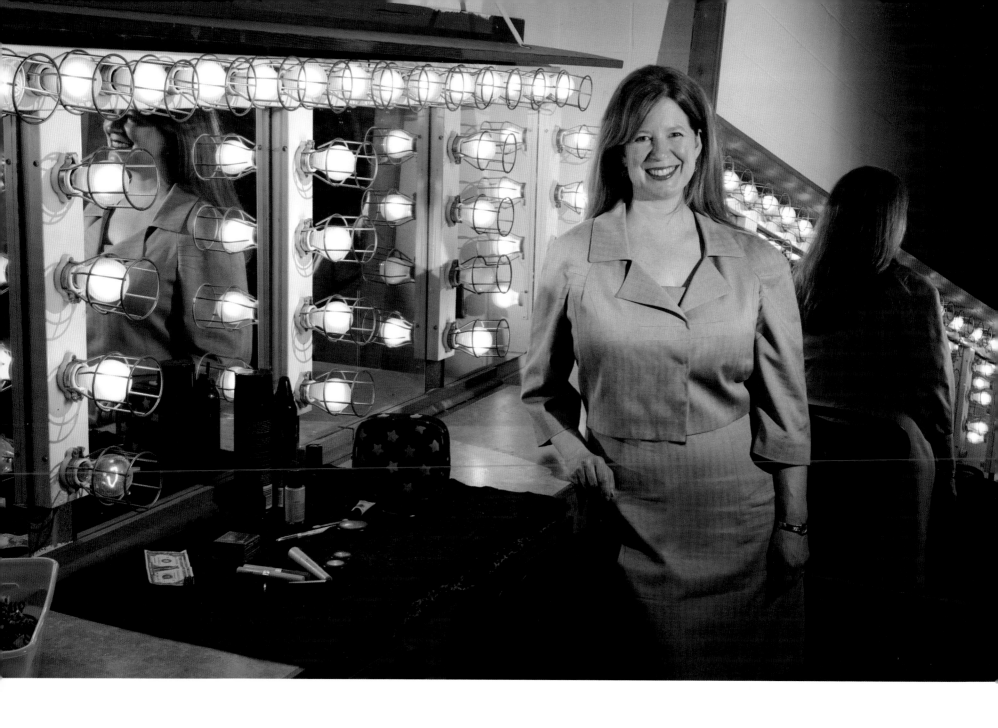

Jennifer Bielstein

Your title of Managing Director of Actors Theatre of Louisville is impressive. What's the work behind the title?

I found my dream job. I work in partnership with the theatre's artistic director. I'm in charge of the theatre's business operations—finance, marketing, fundraising, human resources, information technology, facilities and maintenance, ticket sales, and customer service. A big part of my job is to represent the organization and develop relationships locally and nationally. When I travel around the country as an officer of the League of Resident Theatres, I'm so proud to say that I'm with Actors Theatre.

What attracted you to theatre?

I took a theatre class in high school. I loved it but realized I preferred the business side rather than the stage. I was one of the lucky people who knew early on what I wanted to do with my life—to manage a theatre I admired. Here I am at one of the most amazing theatres in the world.

After living and working in Chicago theatres, what was it like adjusting to a smaller city?

Louisville is an easy place to live your life, and it's extremely supportive of not only Actors Theatre, but the arts in general. In a large city such as Chicago, there's an overwhelming array of choices so it's easy to tune out and not take advantages of some of them. I've found Louisvillians to be very welcoming. And I've been delighted to find that women here really reach out and support each other.

Have you had a particularly memorable experience at Actors Theatre?

One that especially stands out is my first Humana Festival. I had previously attended, but I was elated to finally be part of it all. Seeing several hundred people from all over the world pull together to put on eight plays simultaneously was invigorating and awe-inspiring.

What's your major challenge?

There are so many things competing for people's leisure time. Actors Theatre has to remain relevant and to tell stories in a way that's motivating because theatre is a participatory experience whether you realize it or not. Secondary is the fundraising and the dynamic of being a not-for-profit organization.

Female actors frequently say they aren't offered as many good parts as are their male counterparts. Do you find the theatre industry discriminatory?

I think there is still a gender divide between female and male playwrights and directors, but maybe a little less so in theatre administration.

In a few words, how would you describe yourself?

Hardworking, loyal, and a good friend.

Was there a major factor that shaped your life?

My father's work in the oil industry caused our family to move every two and a half to three years. It was tough, but I became adaptable. I learned how to quickly make friends, and to be open to new experiences and perspectives.

What's the best decision you've made?

The easy answer would be "to move to Louisville." But the best decision I ever made was to pursue a career I'm passionate about.

Is there something people would be surprised to know about you?

I love to play music and dance around the house by myself.

What traits do you most like in a person?

Honesty, directness, empathy, intelligence, and a good sense of humor.

And least?

Dishonesty and manipulativeness.

What haven't you done that you'd like to do?

I have sacrificed family time. I'd like to spend more time with them and my friends.

Is there something you'd like to change about yourself?

I wish I could slow down and worry less. I have long to-do lists, both personally and professionally. I'd like to have more down time and to free up some brain space for intellectual exploration.

What do you most like about yourself?

I like my laugh. I think I have laughed less as I have gotten older, but when I laugh, I laugh heartily.

With which person of note would you most like to spend the day?

The president of the United States, to witness what he experiences every day. I can't imagine having a role in which you'd never be able to please so many people. It would take such a thick skin.

And do you have a thick skin?

It's thick enough, but not incredibly so.

Deborah Blair

Why did you and your husband, Robert, who had been head of school at Kentucky Country Day, give up comfortable, settled lives to open the West End School, an academically rigorous boarding school for middle school boys?

People think it's a big deal that we gave up our home in the East End and came to the West End. That doesn't register with us. Our needs are the needs of the school. We wanted kids in the West End to have the same academic opportunities as the kids on the other side of town. For so many of them, they've lost interest in school and there's no way but down. They have no one to pick them up. They don't realize that it isn't the end of the world as long as they work hard and persevere. Middle school is the tipping point for education and is also the point at which students start to drop off. When students come to us they're already two or three grades behind, but they have every bit the ability of their counterparts in the East End.

You have had tremendous success, but you're also frustrated.

Our graduates are going to some of the finest high schools in the city. They have had more than $2 million in scholarships offered. I'm frustrated because we have the capacity for 24 boys, but we don't have near that many enrolled. We're always trying to figure out how to get more boys in. It's not a traditional "build it and they will come" situation. Quite frankly, we're seen as competition to public schools.

Why was it important to open a boarding school rather than a day school?

It isn't possible to accomplish what the kids need in their lives in six and a half hours a day. But at 24 hours a day you can make a dent. We create our own atmosphere within the walls of the school. It's a safe and stable environment. The kids don't have the day-to-day trials they would have if they didn't live at school; they don't have to worry about hiding from someone who has a gun. What goes on outside of the walls doesn't affect them.

You've created a unique family atmosphere within a very structured environment.

We run a very tight schedule. The kids are either in class or at a meal or in the game room. We're all a family. We eat three meals a day together. Robert and I, and the staff, are the parents, teachers, and guardians. We have a lot of fun. We have a basketball and track team, and we take them on trips.

Does the school have a religious orientation?

It isn't a Christian school, but everything we do is Christian. Most of the kids have a church background and know what we're talking about. Sometimes we have them memorize scripture. In the Bible, there is a section in James about the tongue. In the community where these boys lived, many people use language to tear up each other instead of to raise up each other. We teach that with God's help, they can contain that tongue.

Why do you say the boys are your heroes?

They're giving up their friends, their own computers, televisions, and cell phones to come here to study and learn. They find they have talents they didn't know they have. It's a very challenging atmosphere and they really have to want to be here. Our goal is to return them to the community to be responsible citizens, husbands, and fathers.

When you look back on your life, what do you see?

God has blessed my family. We're pretty easy to get along with; we're usually unruffled. There aren't a lot of highs and lows. We kind of hum along and are low-maintenance. I credit God with sending Robert and me to each other. Our lives are about pleasing God.

What haven't you done that you'd like to do?

Fill the dormitory.

How do you feel about aging?

Aging isn't a big deal. I remember hitting 30 was a real blow. Every decade since then has been easier. I think of myself more like 40 than 67.

What, other than the people in your life couldn't you live without?

My Bible.

Is there anything you would change about yourself if you could?

The quest for becoming more like Jesus, a truly loving person. I'm not. I know all the places I fall short. That grieves me.

Tracy Blue

You and your husband are among Louisville's most successful business people and one of the city's most prominent couples. Your companies rank among the nation's elite. But, separate from your own involvement in those ventures, you have established yourself as a formidable businessperson.

Many people assume Jonathan, my husband, runs *The Voice-Tribune*. That's not true. I'm the publisher and I run it. Following our purchase of the paper, I was involved with it for about a year when I realized it wasn't really going anywhere regarding content. I decided I wanted it to be less newsy and to look more like a magazine. I started making changes and building *The Voice* because I knew it could have a significant impact on the community. I'm trying to use the paper as a way to grow Louisville and make a difference in people's lives. We have a great team in place and produce an excellent product, but I always want next week's paper to be even better.

What's it like to be so involved with your husband in your businesses?

We're good negotiators and we're good partners. We travel well together. We build each other up and complement each other's abilities. And we each accept change in business, marriage, and life.

Are you willing to divulge your nickname?

Sure. An employee gave it to me and it's what my husband and children call me. I'm The Warden. When I say something at home, they usually listen to me and know it's final.

You also seem to run a tight ship at work. Do you see any of yourself in *The Devil Wears Prada*?

I don't think I'm a difficult person to work for, but I admit that I have high expectations. I'm not rigid, but I'm firm. For example, I want the phone answered by the third ring so that it doesn't go to voice mail. I certainly critique what my employees do, but that's because I want them to be creative and to do their best. I want them to feel empowered and to feel good about their work. I believe they have high expectations of themselves.

You seem very driven.

I am driven, but not as much so as my husband. I have a strong, tough side that is balanced by a soft side. I'd do anything for anybody unless they betray me or do anything to my family.

Undoubtedly, there are those who are envious of your wealth and position in the community.

My early life was not at all what it is now. I grew up in a lower-middle-class family. It's very important to me that our children see the world as it really exists. Of course, sometimes they live in a bubble, but I want them to get out of the bubble. The challenge is to raise them properly even though their father is so high-profile. We make a point of taking them places where people aren't as fortunate as are we. Our daughters don't see their lives as anything special compared to other people they know or meet. They don't see race, color, or economic differences.

Does it bother you when your husband is publically or privately criticized about his business dealings or success?

My husband knows everyone in the city and they know him, so he's bound to receive criticism. I have a really thick skin and chalk those comments up to people not understanding a particular situation. Regardless of what they say, I won't say anything negative about them.

Is there anything people would be surprised to know about you?

I'm a very guarded person and would rather spend time at home with my family rather than going out all the time. I used to be intimated by meeting people. However, I'm over that. I'm still working on becoming more comfortable with public speaking and live interviews.

Other than your family and friends, what couldn't you live without?

My faith. While we don't go to synagogue every week and don't say prayers all the time, we live our lives the way the Torah reads.

How do you feel about aging?

I was fine with being 45 years old. But when I turned 46, I told my husband I felt as if my life was over. He told me it was not over and said I should embrace everything about it. But I often think that although the days can be long, time is flying. I told him that one day he will watch his daughters walk down the aisle and will wonder what happened to time. He'll say, "Why didn't you tell me this?" And I'll say, "I did."

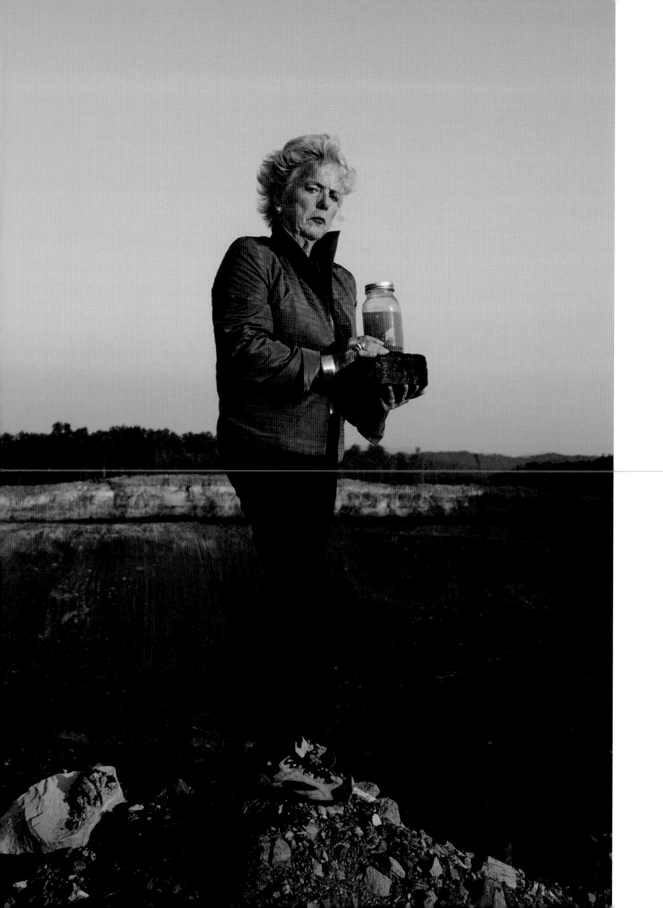

Christy Brown

You're considered one of Louisville's most powerful movers and shakers.
No one does anything alone. People are so complimentary, but if I have been successful it was because I made something fun and interesting to attract a larger number of people to form a consensus and to figure out how to make something happen. The key is to put forth an idea, a concept, or a project and keep massaging it until you're able to achieve results. It's similar to continually molding a piece of clay.

What prompted you to co-found the Cathedral Heritage Foundation (now known as the Center for Interfaith Relations), which led to the Festival of Faiths?
Father Martin Linebach had the brilliant idea to create a festival and condense some of the interfaith programming we were doing at the Cathedral of the Assumption. We invited a wide variety of religious entities. We were thrilled and, quite frankly, amazed at the responses we received. The theme of the first year's festival was the history of Louisville and how particular faiths helped grow the city. The Festival of Faiths has expanded every year, always with a theme. Many of us believe it is a world model yet to be discovered by the world. It affords all of us an opportunity to get out of our individual silos and areas of concentration and cross-fertilize and comingle with others.

You also have had a special bond with Religions for Peace.
It is the world's largest interfaith organization dedicated to stopping war, ending poverty, and protecting the earth. The more my husband and I worked with them at the international level, the more we realized the importance of the work on the local level. We need to inspire our faiths to make our communities stronger, better, and more peaceful.

Much of your work addresses the suffering and violence in the world. Are you optimistic about the future?
We're all inundated minute by minute with tragedies and atrocities, but I believe there are an equal number of miracles happening because of people's kindness and unselfishness. The tagline for *Ode*, one of the best magazines in the world, is "for the intelligent optimist." I would love to have claimed those words. I would like to be an intelligent, optimistic problem solver.

Politics are central to your life. Your involvement in campaigns runs the gamut from the presidential campaigns of Nelson Rockefeller to Bob Dole to John Kerry to Barak Obama. Locally, you've supported John Yarmuth and Greg Fischer. You don't adhere to party lines, do you?
It's not a party thing for me. It's about the best candidate and the best ideas.

You have spent time with Prince Charles on a couple of occasions and think very highly of him.
It's overwhelming what we don't know, and how thoughtless we are about thinking we control it all and know it all. The basic premise of *Harmony: A New Way of Looking at Our World*, by the Prince of Wales, is that we need to understand that nature is an incredible book of learning and that we need to reverse the whole way of looking at Earth. I think Prince Charles is, at the moment, one of the most important global thinkers and leaders. He should be recognized as that. He understands the importance of preservation of all life, natural and human.

What motivates you?
I think we're all here for the purpose of sharing ourselves and caring for others. I'm very blessed to be able to have the time to share myself and to be helpful and, hopefully, to make Louisville a more inspired place. We're all stewards of the earth and I feel a huge responsibility toward that role. When my husband and I married, our first obligation was to create the best marriage we could together and then to be the best parents we could be. Then, whatever time was left was to be contributed to our community.

What's the most important thing you've learned about yourself?
That I have a lot to learn.

You're a member of one of Louisville's wealthiest, most highly visible families. You travel around the world and interact with newsmakers and very famous people. It must be fun to be you.
It is, and I hope the people I work with think it's fun. I decided early on that if I was going to give of myself in civic ways and if others were going to join with me, it had to be fun.

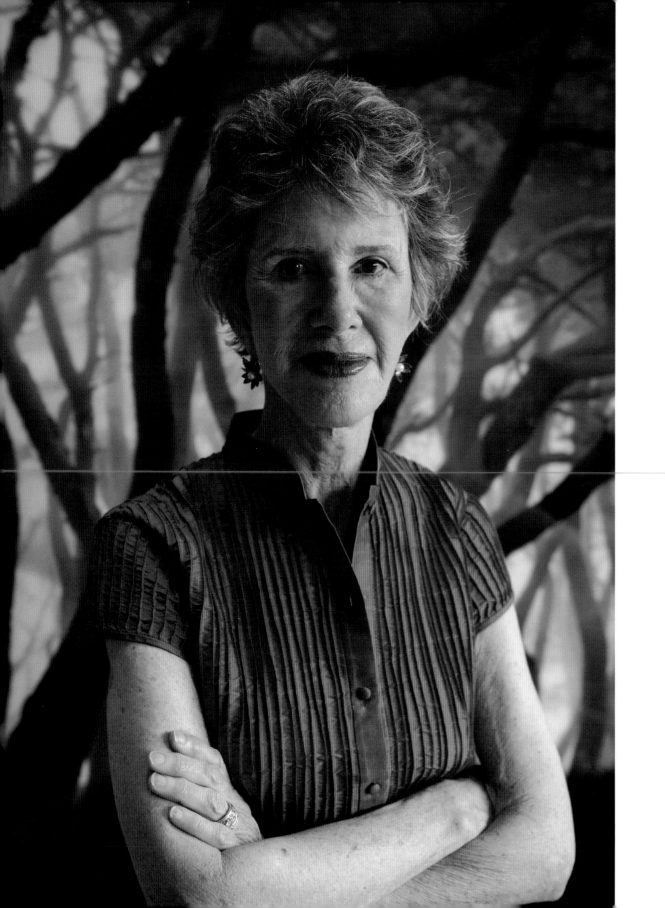

Laura Lee Brown

You're a hotelier, restaurateur, art gallery owner, philanthropist, farmer, and land preservationist. If someone who doesn't know you asks what you do, how do you respond?
I say Steve and I started and own 21C Museum Hotel. That probably initiates a conversation because they haven't a clue.

21C Museum Hotel invites visitors to experience art in an exciting, new way. Why is that so important to you?
Too often people are somewhat intimidated to climb stairways and go between big columns and even have to pay to see art in a museum. At one point we tried to interest the Speed Museum in having a presence downtown for contemporary art, but they felt that running two campuses might be a bit challenging. Steve and I knew people enjoyed our collection at home so we decided to bring it downtown and let people see it. I like the idea that they can have a flush threshold to come in and see art, and that they can do it 24/7 and not have to pay for it. Our art is sometimes provocative and there to ask people to begin to talk about it. We like to see people take part in what we're trying to communicate.

You have made such a visible commitment to downtown Louisville and, at the same time, you live on a farm in Oldham County. Is your heart downtown or on the farm?
We bought the farm to keep it from being developed. Then we had to figure out what to do with it. We love being there. But we also felt that if we were able to vitalize downtown Louisville a little bit, we could interest people to stay downtown and maybe live downtown. By doing that they might not be so interested in pushing development in the country.

Being one of the most social and professional members of the community, do you feel as if you live in a fish bowl?
Not if I keep traveling between the farm and the office. That time allows me to decompress. And I travel out of town quite a bit so the fish bowl gets pretty big.

How do the public and private Laura Lee Brown differ?
There's a lot about me that likes to kick back and read a book or paint or work in my garden or ride a horse. But I gear up to do the things that require me to be more professionally oriented. And I seem to have an energy to lead that life. It's the gearing up and gearing down that probably creates the difference.

What has been the biggest challenge of your life?
I guess it's been learning to live with Steve Wilson. He's extremely creative and has such a remarkable eye. He will often buy art that seems to be over the top and I can't imagine going there. But I have learned to trust his eye. I have learned to temper my own values and tastes to make room for his because they're very sharp.

And your major disappointment?
Probably that we were not able to materialize Museum Plaza.

Other than the people in your life, what couldn't you live without?
Chocolate.

What's the most important thing you've learned about yourself?
To take more time making decisions.

Your list of accomplishments goes on and on. What motivates and inspires you?
A few things. Living on a farm on the river is perhaps the most inspirational. I can always trust it to be there and to do for me what I ask it to do, which is to nail me down to the ground and to the essence of the way I like to lead my life. It is there that I can do so many things that mean heaven to me. Secondly, it's a real high for me when I look at art. I really enjoy collecting art. It's probably an addiction that I have leveled with and pursue with some sort of equilibrium. Finally, painting and photography are other resources of excitement for me and are a passion.

Is there anything that intimidates you?
I'm not happy around spiders. But I tolerate them, give them their space, and don't want to kill them.

If you could be anywhere in the world right now, where would you be and what would you be doing?
I might be in London looking at art.

What's next for you?
Not retirement. I think it's developing more 21C Museum Hotels. That might seem like what I'm already doing, but each one is very different.

Finish the sentence, "I wish women would…
recognize their strengths."

Vickie Yates Brown

As co-chair of the health law practice group of Frost Brown Todd, president and CEO of Nucleus, and one of the city's most powerful and influential individuals, you seem to have shattered the proverbial glass ceiling.

My life would not be a good example to gauge that against. Life is about choices. I haven't had to make choices that a lot of women have had to make. I don't have children so I wasn't trying to balance husband, children, and a career. I singularly focused on my career.

Do you ever regret that decision?

I try not to look back. I believe God has a hand in your life. I'm not going to second guess. Would I love to have had children? Yes. But I feel blessed to have a wonderful stepdaughter.

Why did you decide to concentrate on health law?

Healthcare just happened for me. After clerking for a Kentucky Supreme Court justice following graduation from law school, I joined a small law firm that had a healthcare focus. I quickly got into that niche. It's an exciting field because it's still evolving and encompasses so many political, ethical, and legal issues. Being in the middle of the mix, and making policy and law, is stressful but rewarding. It's bigger than myself or any one person. I almost feel it's a calling and that I was put in this place for a specific purpose.

Nucleus is making national headlines. It's not a simple concept to define because of its complexity.

It's a support-based environment where scientists and researchers come together to commercialize ideas and create economic success stories. Our tenants and partnerships capture a diversity of fields, including healthcare, lifelong wellness and aging care, engineering, energy, applied sciences, information technology, life sciences, medical devices, logistics, nanotechnology, and advanced manufacturing, among others.

To achieve your level of success, do you need to be an Alpha dog and have a Type A personality?

I'm very goal-oriented. It's more about being tenacious than being aggressive. I'll move mountains to try to make something happen. I usually function as a collaborator and facilitator rather being the Alpha dog. But I don't give up.

What drives you?

The way I was raised. I had great female role models. My mother was a very take-control kind of person, as was her mother. My mother was the overseer on our farm. I grew up seeing women in men's roles. Our family friend Gladys Williams Black was the first female county attorney in Kentucky. She mentored me from the beginning and wanted me to eventually take over her practice and become the county attorney. With role models like those, it wasn't an option to sit around and have someone take care of me. At the time, I thought I'd grow up to be a farmer and a lawyer.

Are you still kind of a farm girl at heart?

I'd love to spend more time farming and gardening on the family farm. We're growing lots of heirloom fruits and vegetables.

You've said your friends might want to throw away some of the Christmas gifts you've given them.

Years ago my family taught me how to can and preserve. I can the whole continuum of vegetables and fruits, and especially like to preserve asparagus, apple butter, strawberry jam, and brandied peaches and cherries. I've proudly given them as Christmas presents. Finally I took an eye-opening class in home-based processing and learned how it's supposed to be done to ensure the food remains safe. I must say I had not always done it the right way. I'm surprised some of my gifts weren't deadly. I found out that it's more dangerous to can vegetables than it is fruits. It's hard to kill someone with jam, so now I give away only canned fruit. Chow Chow? I'm not going there anymore.

For a while you had a budding future as a columnist.

I wouldn't go that far! I wrote a column, Vickie's Victuals, for the *Spencer Magnet* newspaper in Spencer County. Hardly anyone knew victuals is the legal term for vittles.

What would people be surprised to know about you?

How tender-hearted and sensitive I am. I can get my feelings hurt at the drop of a hat. I try to cover it, because as a lawyer you're supposed to be tough.

Martha Calderwood

What was your "aha!" moment that led you to become a teacher?

During my sophomore year of college I was in a large world literature class. I had the chance to explain the *Allegory of the Cave* to the class. I remember thinking, "I really want them to understand this." I thought that must be what teaching is about. Everything after that fit into place.

How were the opportunities available to women different than they are now?

I was the first in my family to go to college. Going to college just wasn't what females did growing up in Central Pennsylvania. Most of them grew up and got married. Women at that time could be teachers, secretaries, or nurses. My class was on the front edge of the baby boomers. It was exciting that I was able to grow up in the period when things were starting to open up for women. I'm not a raging feminist, but I had more opportunities than even my older sister.

You've had some incredible travel experiences.

A few of the trips I remember most are those to the Galapagos, two summers in Maine, and the trip to Greece when I drove a mini-bus with 14 students all around Delphi, Pylos, Corinth, and Mycennae.

I went to China to conduct a training session for Chinese teachers of English in Jiujian. It was some of the hardest teaching I've ever done. I'm used to having about 20 students in a class, but I had 60 to 90 teachers in each class. I talked about how they could introduce their students to Walt Whitman's *I Hear America Singing*, the Gettysburg Address, and Martin Luther King, Jr.'s I Have a Dream speech. I asked them to construct *I Hear China Singing*. They wrote such remarkable poems fashioned after that. It was finally a breakthrough. It gives me chills to think about it. I also taught about 150 people in Jiujian how to dance.

I made some very good friends while I was teaching American literature in Germany. The German students were a very hard sell. They'd ask probing questions and were good thinkers.

You've received several awards for distinguished teaching. What makes you such a good teacher?

I love what I do and that translates to the kids. They know I'm completely invested in teaching. To me, it's not a job. If it ever gets to be a job, I'll stop. I don't like giving students the answer. I set up my lessons so they have to connect the dots. I like high school kids because you can talk to them like people. I enjoy the way they look at life. They really do listen to you but they also know a fake when they see one.

An archeological dig is a fun vacation for you, isn't it?

I went on a dig through Earth Watch, an organization that takes volunteers all over the world. I was supposed to work on a Bronze Age sanctuary in Majorca, but I injured my knee. They sent me to Switzerland to look for plateosaurus that probably had fallen into a swamp.

Some people talk about their hippie days. You say you're still a hippie.

You never grow out of it because your mindset is still there. There are so many experiences I vividly remember from that time. I'll never forget seeing Charles de Gaulle and Haile Selassie walking down the street together in JFK's funeral procession. I also marched in Washington. I was an activist then. Am I a liberal? Probably. I'm not ashamed to say it.

You have such varied interests!

I enjoy sailing, weaving on a floor loom, folk music, and cycling. I'm not frantic, but I'm busy. There's so much more I want to do. I'd like to learn to play the bagpipes. I want to see some of Africa. I believe I will eventually go to Narusha, Tanzania, as a mentor to their teachers. And I want to go to Morocco, and down the Nile on a boat.

How do you feel about getting older?

My mother was, and still is, a role model for me. Her longevity, fortitude, and courage continue to amaze me. She's taught me how to age. Part of aging is the revelation of who you are. I'm not afraid to get old. It seasons you. There's a reason that process happens.

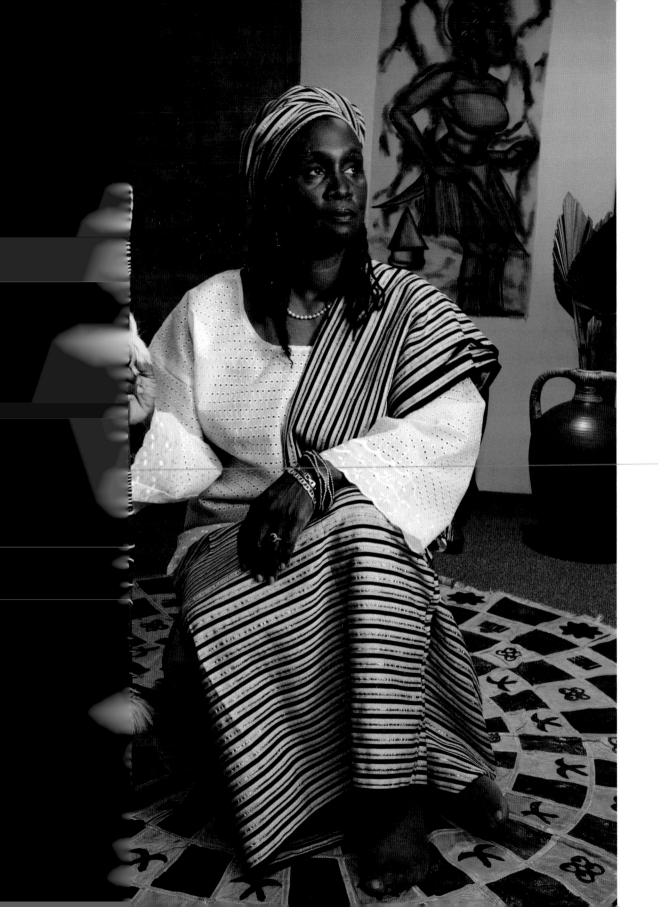

Dr. Renée
Campbell

Yours is a multifaceted life. Here you're pictured in your role as an African chief.
As a little girl, I never imagined I would be an African chief. I didn't grasp the true story of Africa until I was in my twenties. I had only heard about Africa in connection to slavery. When I began discovering and exploring the history and culture of Africa, I wanted to go the motherland. On my first trip to Ghana, in West Africa, the people immediately embraced me and I knew I had a purpose there. Having a social-work background, I became involved with the Girls' Growth and Development program, which was developed to help girls learn a skill so they could start a business.

By the second time I went to Africa, I was being considered to be a subchief in Tolon, one of the largest villages in Ghana, and one of the poorest with the most street children. I was given the name Maltinaa and was assigned the role of development chief, appropriate since I'm a social worker. At the ritual during which I became chief, I was askinned, meaning the village chiefs, the Queen Mother, officials, and dignitaries witnessed the occasion as I was dressed in my chief garb. Members of the Tolon/Kumbùngu tribe, a warrior tribe, followed behind me, dancing and drumming. It was a spiritual experience, as if I was being born again. When I return for visits, dancers and drummers follow me everywhere. Villagers address me as Chief and are not allowed to get very close to me. My staff serves as my security. I'm not allowed to carry anything by myself. Someone follows me with pillows to sit on when I visit from hut to hut. I'm constantly fanned because it's so hot. It took some time to get used to all of that, but everyone needs that kind of love!

My job as chief is to empower the women in the village, to facilitate educational resources and, ultimately, to build a school. I'm working with the Girls' Growth and Development entrepreneurial program and am also involved with work focusing on domestic violence.

You're also President and CEO of Wesley House, in Louisville. Your mission there is varied and complex.
Wesley House helps people help themselves. We provide child care and computer education for displaced workers and people who want to get off public assistance and to obtain a marketable skill. Wesley House serves a large immigrant population. Hispanics and Latinos make up 42 percent of our clients. We also sponsor a gently used clothing store and, as part of the Louisville Asset Coalition, enable individuals to become more financially literate and assist them with income tax preparation.

Domestic violence and abuse are target program areas of Wesley House.
Yes, because they are so prevalent and so complex. One of every three girls, and one of every seven boys, is in some way abused before they reach the age of 18. Shocking statistics show that when a woman upgrades her skills or becomes employed, domestic violence in her home begins or increases. One out of every seven men is in an abusive relationship in which the woman is the abuser. It makes sense that when we're serving families that we have a component that addresses these issues. My staff is trained in intervention, prevention, and assessment of family violence and abuse.

Women in domestic violence and abusive situations are often criticized for not leaving the situation. How do you react to that?
I know that belief is coming from ignorance, so I don't get mad. I try to explain that there's a reason a woman stays in an abusive or violent home, and emphasize that no woman wants to be abused. There are layers and layers of reasons why she feels like she can't leave. It probably began when she was a little girl, what she saw her mother go through, what she thinks is expected of women. She may still be living in the honeymoon stage, which is when the man says he's sorry, that he'll never do it again. That scenario rarely plays out.

In three or four words, how would you describe yourself?
Strong, loving, committed, and sincere.

What do you like best about yourself?
I don't let anyone tell me I can't do something I think is important to do. They may not have the vision or the faith that I do, so I hit the "Delete" button and act like they didn't say it.

And least?
It makes me uncomfortable when I'm perceived as quiet and shy. In reality, I'm being reserved and thoughtful. I don't want to speak unless I have something to say.

Kathy Cary

You were a guest chef on Martha Stewart's show. What did you think of her?

She was tough to work with. She lacked manners and had a wimpy handshake!

As chef at the former Fig Tree and now as chef/owner of Lilly's— A Kentucky Bistro, you put Louisville on the culinary map and elevated local dining to a new level. Where did your love of food and cooking begin?

In my family's kitchen. I learned from my mother and two wonderful women who worked for us, Lydia and Courtney. Courtney was a wonderful pastry chef and cook. As a young child, I loved peeling peaches and watching them become peach cobbler, and watching magic as flour turned into yeast rolls. I participated in picking cherries and apples and tomatoes. I also learned so much from the early days of *Gourmet* magazine. I developed an appreciation of good food, from basic fried chicken to those things I learned when traveling and experimenting with different foods.

Why was being the chef at the Fig Tree such a challenge?

After opening my own catering company and later working as a lunch chef for a restaurant in Washington, D.C., I was hired as the Fig Tree's executive chef at the age of 21. Most of my kitchen staff were older men. Some of them didn't particularly like it that their boss was a young woman who didn't have much experience in the restaurant business. I was weaving my French cooking experience into the menu but also did fried chicken and corn pudding. The menu changed every day for lunch and every two weeks for dinner. The hours and work were grueling. The owners were enjoying making a profit off me and weren't appreciating what I was doing. I decided if I was going to work that hard, it was going to be for me.

But you didn't immediately open Lilly's.

In the interim I was fashion director for Stewart's department store. I also taught cooking classes and catered.

You're widely recognized for your French-inspired use of traditional Kentucky ingredients with contemporary twists. Isn't that a difficult melding of ingredients and technique?

Not at all. Growing up on a farm had a tremendous influence on me. It was a terrific experience to pick the food, to feel the dirt on your feet, and to have the reward of harvesting something you've planted. French cuisine was a perfect fit with that because it has always had an emphasis on fresh ingredients. Farmers' markets and knowing where food comes from have always been a part of my life, and I'm thrilled that such interest is blossoming here and around the country.

You're quite the gardener yourself.

I'm proud of my garden although I have a lot to learn about gardening. It's my therapy and it's good exercise. I love the beauty of living plants. They kind of like me. They just keep growing and don't talk back.

Rumor is that you've never had a Big Mac. Surely that's not true!

I've never had one in my entire life. I have no desire. In fact, the idea almost makes me cringe.

Lilly's is a Louisville icon. What makes it so successful?

Good food and great service go hand in hand. We've fought to be a neighborhood restaurant, not a destination restaurant. One friend said, "This is my tavern." It was the best compliment I've ever had. There's no dress code. We have a warm ambience. We have tablecloths not because Lilly's is fancy, but because we have ugly tables. It's also little things such as having the wine list printed on the back of the menu. It isn't as intimidating as a six-page wine book. There are no candles on the tables. I think they are passé. I'd rather have candles in the window than a dumb candle on the table. (And there was the time two people caught their menus on fire.)

What inspires you?

Reading — not just cookbooks, but novels, too. I also like to read menus that customers bring back from their travels. It's a great way to see what's going on around the country and around the world, and to see if we're on the right track.

What do you like best about yourself?

My discipline and work ethic.

And least?

That same work ethic. Maybe I take on more than I can handle.

Elaine Chao

What has been the biggest challenge in your life?

Coming to America as an immigrant and learning how to adapt, adjust, and assimilate to a new country, new culture, new language, new food, new people, and a new way of thinking.

I came as a young child at the age of eight, not speaking a word of English. Incredibly positive, hardworking, courageous, and self-reliant, my parents forged a new destiny for our family. Born in China, they grew up in the tragedy that was twentieth-century Chinese history—a period marked by societal upheaval, civil wars, and foreign invasions. In 1949, at the height of the Chinese civil war, my parents made their separate ways to Taiwan. There, they met, married, started a family and a new life together.

My father was a young man with ability and dreams. Yet he knew that he would not have many opportunities in the Old World. So, he pursued advanced education. In Taiwan, examinations were given on a national basis. He took the national examination and not only did he score number one but he broke all the previous records, which were both huge accomplishments. He was written up in all the newspapers and the Taiwan government granted him permission to go to America.

The opportunity to go to America was so rare that my father left right away, even though my mother was seven months pregnant with their third child. Our family endured three long years of separation before my father was able to bring my mother, my two sisters, and me to America.

We came to America on a cargo ship, an ocean journey that took 37 days. Our initial years were very difficult as my father worked three jobs to make ends meet. We lived in a small one-bedroom apartment. My mother, the pillar of our family, scrimped and saved and made our home a haven of solace, tranquility, and love.

Because of these experiences, I understand what it feels like to not be a part of the mainstream community, and how frightening life can sometimes appear. This has spurred me to public service to help others access greater opportunities to improve their lives.

What has been your major disappointment?

I've always been a positive, forward-looking person. Once I've overcome a challenge, I don't really go back and dwell upon it. I try to learn from the experience and hope that as I am tested, I will become a better and more compassionate person.

What's the most important thing you've learned about yourself?

That I can't do it all by myself. Fortunately, I have been blessed with a great husband, family, friends, and colleagues.

What haven't you done that you would like to do?

I'd like to promote legacy projects that help others remember the contribution of the previous generation and how lucky we are to be living in this country.

Is there anything people would be surprised to know about you?

One, I'm a huge sci-fi fan. And, two, I love campaigning. It gives me a chance to travel throughout the state and visit with the wonderful people in our beautiful Commonwealth. I've lived in so many places in my life. When I came to Kentucky, I felt that I had come home.

What, other than the people in your life, couldn't you live without?

Not much. I have pretty simple tastes. I have a pretty simple lifestyle. I don't really attach myself to material things.

Candyce Clifft

For a while it looked as if you were going to be standing behind a pharmacy counter, but now you're in front of Fox 41 television cameras every day.
I was always fascinated by the news, but I studied to be a pharmacist. My lightbulb moment occurred when I was sitting in a college organic chemistry class. The light shone from heaven and said, "What are you doing in here? This isn't for you." I knew I was in the wrong place and decided to switch to journalism.

Isn't television news very competitive, and a bit of a dog-eat-dog world?
I've never felt it to be a cutthroat business because the people at other stations in Louisville are cordial, kind, and respectful. The business is perfect for me because I like digging for facts, telling stories, and meeting interesting people. And it's very rules-oriented, which appeals to me.

You've covered many major stories? Which ones particularly stand out in your mind?
My first big story was the UPS strike. I also covered the school shooting in Paducah. And the Karen Sypher/Rick Pitino story was, of course, very big. I had the memorable interview with her. That was a team effort. Our staff had meeting after meeting about that story to be sure we were aggressive enough, but also fair.

Is it difficult to separate yourself from stories that are controversial or emotional?
I separate the news from my life. If I really sat and thought about all the emotional stories I've covered, I'd be a very depressed person. When I go home, I'm Candyce Clifft, wife and mother, not Candyce Clifft, news anchor.

What has been the most significant accomplishment of your life?
I took up running in my mid-thirties, just a few years ago. I had never run more than a mile in my life, and that year I worked up to half marathons. It was one of the hardest things I have ever done. It took a lot of dedication and positive thinking and encouraging myself. I'm really proud of it.

Other than the people in your life, what couldn't you live without?
My faith. Chocolate is a close second.

What's the most important life lesson you have learned?
There are really two things. While we're young, we like to think we can change the world, but as we get older we realize some things are out of our control.

I don't get upset over things I can't control. The other important thing I have learned relates to my Type A personality. Even as a child I was very driven. I used to think that if a newsperson wasn't working for a network, he or she hadn't arrived. But I have matured to understand that success isn't just a title. There are positions like mine that might pay more money or be more prestigious in a larger city, but having one of those jobs is not my definition of success. Having a family and working with nice people in a city I love are the things I cherish.

Is there one word that best describes you?
Dependable. People know they can count on me. I like that about myself. However, it does cause me to occasionally bite off more than I can chew.

What do you like best about yourself?
I'm a pretty low-maintenance person.

What would you like to change about yourself?
I'd have more patience. And, I push everything to the last minute. I think that's the way I'm wired.

Is there anything people would be surprised to know about you?
As a child, I didn't like to read. My job requires me to read out loud all the time. But I only started to read for pleasure in the last five or six years.

Who is your hero?
My husband heads the list. I know dads' roles have changed over the years, but I would wager that he's involved more than most fathers. One minute he's helping with homework and the next minute he's in the yard playing with the kids. And he's so creative and has unlimited patience.

How do you feel about aging?
I want to try and stay healthy and take care of myself. I'm not beyond a good moisturizer, but I have no plans for plastic surgery because it's not who I am. I'll have to do the best with what I've got. It's natural to look older. I think you are ridiculous when you try to fight it.

Is there anything in your life that you regret?
No. I believe in the power of prayer. My life has been one blessing after another.

Ruth Cloudman

You recently retired as Chief Curator and Mary and Barry Bingham, Sr. Curator of European and American Art at the Speed Museum. That sounds glamorous. But it must have been very intense. What were your major challenges?

That's true, often it was intense. If you are passionate about what you do, work can be intense, but at the end of the day, that's a great thing.

And major accomplishments?

I'm really grateful to have had the chance to help bring great art to our community whether through acquiring major works of art for the collection, such as the paintings by Paul Cézanne, Jacob van Ruisdael, and Alfred Sisley, presenting important exhibitions, or even giving lectures that excited people about art.

Is the museum world a good field for women, or is there a glass ceiling?

The art world has really changed. Three decades ago, there were very few female museum directors and chief curators. Now women are in top positions at many museums.

How has technology changed people's appreciation of art?

People's access to images of works of art has been enhanced exponentially by technology and the Internet. When I'm traveling, before visiting a new museum, I visit their website to see what they have on view. That way I can plan my visit and enjoy anticipating the great things I'm going to see. (I also check out the online menus of restaurants I'll be going to!) Online access to art is a great tool, but people will always love the real thing. There's nothing like actually standing in front of a great work of art.

Even as a child, were you interested in art?

Oh, yes. My parents collected a little, mainly 18th-century furniture and pottery and porcelain, with the occasional painting, and I joined them on their collecting expeditions. They also took me regularly into New York City to the museums when we lived in Westchester County. My favorite was the Metropolitan Museum. I also liked to paint and draw as a kid and found my happy place in my elementary school's art studio.

You travel throughout the world, but you have a special fondness for Kentucky, don't you?

Yes, one reason I love Louisvillians and Kentuckians is because they are so warm, friendly, and hospitable. Also, Kentucky retains roots in the 18th century and I appreciate that sense of history.

Do you have a bucket list?

Yes, and high on it is seeing a female president of the United States in my lifetime.

Do you think you've "found" yourself?

I think I find myself a little every day. I'm a learner and can look back and see how I've changed, how I analyze and look at things differently now than I did years ago. One of the most important things I have learned is to strive for balance in life.

You seem very self-assured. What intimidates you?

Many things intimidate me but I've also realized that certain situations that most intimidated me initially turned out to be great experiences in the end. That's been encouraging.

Finish the sentence, "If I could change one thing about myself, I would...
bark less and wag more."

Do you have a secret indulgence?

Yes, but it's a secret only to those who haven't met me yet—my Pomeranians Teddy and Tiger.

Jef Conner

Your co-founding Ronald McDonald House of Louisville was the result of a personally devastating experience.

My daughter was born with stage four neuroblastoma, a rare form of cancer. She had radical surgery four days later, followed by massive radiation. There have been many complications but she leads a normal life and is now a mother.

While she was in the hospital, someone dropped off a copy of *Reader's Digest* that had an article about a Ronald McDonald House that had opened in Philadelphia. I was so intrigued because I was meeting so many families, unlike ours, who had traveled far from home and had nowhere to stay while their critically ill children were being treated. Parents often had to sleep in the halls of the hospital because they had no affordable option. I wrote to Ray Kroc, the founder of McDonald's, and explained that I wanted to open a Ronald McDonald House in Louisville. He sent me a personal check for $12,500. That and establishing a wonderful relationship with Louisville oncologist Dr. Sal Bertolone got things off to a great start. People from all over the community showed they had huge hearts and became dedicated to the project. I found out what a giving spirit there is in Louisville.

McDonald's has been a phenomenal supporter from the very beginning here in Louisville and throughout the country. We made a presentation to a group of employees at GE for $50,000 to be used for heating and cooling and washers and dryers. They said, "Can't we do more?" The relationship with GE was cemented and led to the company's involvement with Ronald McDonald Houses in other cities.

I think one of the reasons our fundraising was so successful is that instead of targeting one or two large donors, we brought in many, many smaller donors. When we opened in 1984 we had absolutely no debt.

That was a great beginning, but there's much more to the Louisville Ronald McDonald House story.

We opened Ronald McDonald family rooms at Kosair Children's Hospital, Norton Suburban Hospital, and Frazier Rehabilitation Institute. In 2003 we opened the third-floor expansion of Ronald McDonald House, and in 2009 completed the fourth-floor expansion. We now have 36 rooms, including two immune-suppressed suites.

McDonald's recognized your success and sought your expertise for their charitable activities.

I was honored that McDonald's offered me a position on their foundation board for Ronald McDonald Houses, as well as on an international advisory board.

Volunteerism is a major part of your life.

The many volunteer opportunities I have had in my adult life have blessed me and brought me so much joy. I'm passionate about exploring ways to assist the homeless in a positive, constructive way, and I have valued my volunteer experiences in this realm, such as at Wayside Christian Mission. I think the big question we have to ask ourselves is, "Are we really helping the homeless by the way we serve them now, or are we warehousing them?" There are thousands of homeless people in Louisville. Instead of building more shelters, we have to get to the root of the problem.

We also have to help homeless individuals in a real, immediate way. I was very moved when I read about a 4-H girl in West Virginia who was worried about children who live in homeless shelters but don't have even a suitcase. Inspired by that, through Southeast Christian Church we organized an effort to distribute in one year more than 2,000 suitcases that had clothing, personal hygiene items, reading material, and other necessities. The second time we distributed about 2,800 filled suitcases. That just shows what people can do when they come together to address an issue.

What would you like to do that you haven't done?

Write a historical fiction series.

Do you have any regrets?

I regret not being a serious student and not taking advantage of all the wonderful teachers I had through my life.

What traits do you most admire in people?

Hands down, I appreciate honesty and dependability.

When you look into the future, what do you see for yourself?

I don't know how much better life could be for me.

Karen Conner

You're captain of Louisville Fire and Rescue. Did you want to be a firefighter when you were a little girl?

I never had any intention of joining the fire department until someone came into the sports store where I worked and suggested I apply. I made it on the first try. If I had had a whim that this job was as cool as it is, I would have joined in my 20s.

Tell us the real story of being a female firefighter.

It will always be an old boys' network. There were some issues at first, but then they figured out I would chew their ass just like the next guy. There are women on the job who don't have any problems, and there are women who don't get along so well with the guys. It depends more on the girl than on the guy. I have never filed a complaint. I handle things my own way. When I came to this station as captain, one of the men told me the guys were afraid of me because they were worried they would have to change their demeanor and would have to be careful what they said and how they said it. But they don't have to act that way with me. I probably cuss worse than they do.

You went to school to become a veterinarian, and describe those four years as a disaster.

I was working at a vet clinic and decided to go to vet school. One day I was at the University of Kentucky's agriculture farm for a class. The people around me were wearing boots with buckles the size of my head. They put a long glove on my arm and told me to stick my arm in a cow's ass to feel around. That was just too much. To make matters worse, I had already dropped my notebook in a pig trough (not the food trough, but the excrement trough). I didn't want to have to copy all those notes so I had to put up with the stench every day. Finally, I went to the admin office and told them I was transferring to kinesiology. I was switching to exercise.

What's the most important lesson you've learned?

People shock the hell out of me every day. Just when you think you've seen it all, someone will come up with something new. Never get used to the norm. You could be in the grocery store and an old lady bitches you out. It's happened to me.

Is there anything people would be surprised to know about you?

That I studied dance for 20 years. Even people who know me would be shocked to know that I wore tights and got on a stage. They know me as a rugby player, not anything remotely feminine.

What have been the most significant accomplishments of your life?

Getting this job and being the only chick in drill school. It was a very militant, Army-style boot camp. After the other woman dropped out, it was 30 guys and me. The other accomplishment would be having children. Pregnancy was awful and childbirth was an amazing feat. I wasn't wanted around the firehouse while I was pregnant, so I had nothing to do. I put on a respirator and painted every room in the house. I was kicked off the roof for cleaning gutters when I was five months pregnant.

And the biggest challenge?

Juggling the mom thing with the job. I drop off the face of the earth for 24 hours every third day. But on the upside, career day at my kids' school is really cool. Some other kid will bring a banker parent, but I come with the helmet and the ax.

What's the most important thing you've learned about yourself?

That I'm potentially the most patient person my friends have met. I can put up with an insane amount of bullcrap from someone, or everyone can be freaking out around me, but I'm okay.

How would you finish the sentence, "I wish women would…

get off their asses and become more confident." I hate walking into a business office that has called in a fire alarm and be looked at like a zoo animal. But what bothers me more is when it comes from a woman. That drives me insane. I hate it when women think they can't do things. I wish I had a quarter for every time a woman looks at me in uniform and asks, "Do they (the firefighters at the station) make you cook all the time?"

Mary Craik

You had a difficult childhood. People could be very cruel to you when you were young.

I grew up in a place where we had an outhouse. Then I lived in the projects and then in a trailer. People called me trash.

You enrolled in college when you were 27 years old. And you decided to learn to paint when you were 75. Exploring new paths and never giving up seem to define much of your life. What has inspired you to keep evolving?

I have always been a high-energy person who was easily bored. As one phase of my life ended, I needed to find something to replace it. My mother gave me self-confidence. She made me believe I was special and could do anything. I was always interested in other people's art but never dreamed I could be an artist until I became a caretaker to my husband for many years and wanted to do something with my time until he died.

"Feminism" wasn't part of most people's vocabularies when you started paving the way for reform. What were some of the most painful and difficult challenges you encountered in your own journey and in that of helping other women?

I became a feminist in 1965. I had a master's degree and was a research assistant in the Office of Instructional Studies at the University of Texas at El Paso. The president of the university had to fill out a questionnaire on projected job needs. The form had job titles and there were separate columns for males and females. He told me to put zeros in the female column except for jobs for maids and secretaries. I decided to leave and get a Ph.D.

You're one of the region's most respected fiber artists. Why did you choose fiber art instead of another form of artistic expression?

I made my first dress when I was 8 years old. I have sewed all my life. I could make fabric do what I wanted it to do, so I decided to make contemporary quilted wall hangings.

In what ways are artists different from the rest of us?

I think everyone is an artist. They just don't know it.

What have been the biggest challenges in your life?

Helping get rid of racism and sexism. And bringing a class-action lawsuit against St. Cloud State University.

And your major disappointments?

That I still live in a racist, sexist world. Having it take nine years to win the lawsuit. And the death of my husband of fifty-nine years.

What's been the most significant accomplishment of your life?

Establishing the Mary Craik Scholarship for Women at the University of Louisville.

What's the most important thing you've learned about yourself?

I do not give up. I keep going until I accomplish my goal.

Is there anything that intimidates you?

I don't let anyone intimidate me.

What do you like best about yourself?

That I care about other people.

And least?

That I lack patience.

What's your biggest regret?

When I was a junior in high school, I was given the opportunity to skip my senior year and participate in an experimental program at the University of Louisville. I regret that I didn't take the offer.

About what do you worry the most?

I worry most about my health. At 88 years old, my body is falling apart.

How would you finish the sentence, "I wish women would…

get together nationwide and fight for their rights (scream, march, write, and do anything legal) in an organized way to get the country's attention and to get an Equal Rights Amendment."

Tammy York Day

You have attributed your participation in Leadership Kentucky and Leadership Louisville as key to your success as an executive with Delta Dental. Why were they so influential?

The experiences were incredible. We visited cities throughout the state, interviewed death row inmates at Eddyville, studied the correlation between a lack of education and crime, went into a coal mine, and met with the governor and legislators. We had the same level of involvement, but in different ways, in Louisville. It all helped me understand how to more effectively guide our foundation and how it can make such a difference in individuals' lives.

Your name and community involvement go hand in hand.

Our mother took us to volunteer with her, even on Christmas Day, when we were kids. I remember one Christmas at the Lord's Kitchen, a soup kitchen, we were giving out gifts. By the time we got to an older gentleman, we were out of gifts. "That's okay, I'm too old anyway," he said. I cried on the way home and began to realize that we all have such a responsibility to help those who need it.

Much of your nonprofit work involves glittering events. Do you ever worry that you're known as a party girl rather than as an executive?

I have found that some people may be quick to form an opinion about me without knowing me. I'm cognizant of it but I don't worry about it because I'm so proud of the contributions the events with which I'm associated are making to the people and the city.

In a few words, how would you describe yourself?

Witty, intelligent, impatient, and kind.

What do you like best about yourself?

I have a very outgoing personality. I like that I'm straightforward and that you always know where you stand with me. And I'm a warm person. I can make people feel comfortable in any situation.

What traits do you most like in others?

I appreciate people being forthright and considerate.

And least?

I can't stand passive-aggressive or mean-spirited people. I've found that while they're few and far between, some are just mean-spirited, and that's the way it is.

Is there anything that intimidates you?

No.

There must have been several defining moments in your life. Which ones would you like to share?

Certainly the death of my mother. She, my sister, and I were a unit and were very close. And going through busing was very difficult but it ended up being a good experience. Meeting people we've helped through community work and seeing how the money we've raised has impacted their lives continues to impact and inspire me.

Do you have a bucket list?

I want to travel to all seven continents.

What's the best decision you ever made?

I married well. My husband is intelligent and funny and is an extremely good person. He isn't as social as I am, but we balance each other.

You're very open about the things you've learned.

I've had to learn not to fight every battle like it's my last. I now know that I have to pick and choose the battles. But I still have to figure out how to help people approach new ventures that aren't understood and to convince them to branch out of their comfort zones in their business and personal lives.

Other than the people in your life, what couldn't you live without?

My dogs and cats. They're my babies. At one time I had a miniature horse and a Scottish Highland cow. My friends call me Tammy Doolittle.

What has been the most significant accomplishment in your life?

I was a late college graduate. I went to school for two years and then took a 17-year hiatus so I could move for career opportunities. I graduated with a business degree while working full time and chairing boards and community organizations.

Is there anything you would change about yourself if you could?

I have struggled with weight. I'm never going to be skinny.

Do you think you've "found" yourself?

I'm pleased but not satisfied. I don't think I'll ever be satisfied.

How do you feel about aging?

Sometimes when I look in the mirror and see another line or wrinkle, I think it might be nice to be 20 again. But aging really doesn't bother me. I wouldn't trade my experiences for youth. Would I consider cosmetic surgery? Sure, if I get to the point that I feel like I need it.

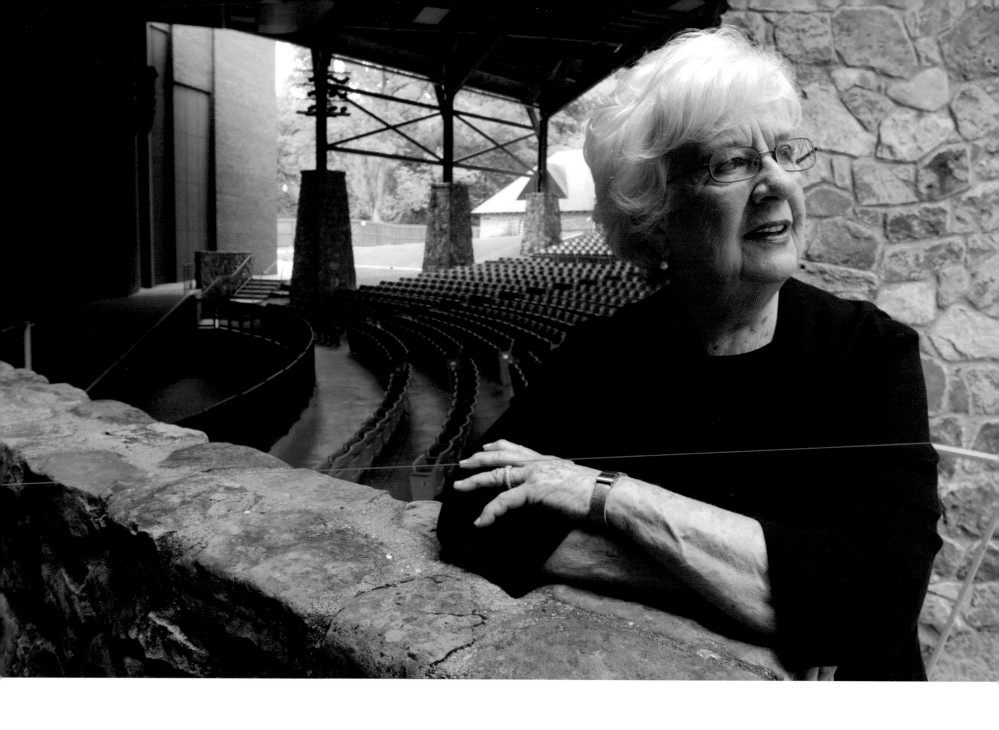

Dolores Delahanty

You were on the Catholic Wall of Shame. That's quite a distinction.
I'm a Catholic. I testified for prochoice legislature. People would, and still do, use language to inappropriately stir up things. The crux of the issue is whether a fetus is a person at the time of conception. I think there are earlier moral issues—the dignity of an individual, self-determination, and the right to make choices. Because of my belief in the right of a woman to control her own body, I was placed on the Wall of Shame.

But the right to choose certainly isn't the only women's issue with which you've been involved.
I had marched for civil rights and had done things to express my concern about equal rights for all people, but I hadn't figured out how women could achieve control of their own lives. I co-founded the Kentucky Women's Political Caucus to encourage women to take a look at their political involvement. I became president of the National Women's Education Fund because I thought it was imperative that women be encouraged to run for office. I was also chair of the legislative committee of the Kentucky Commission on Women. One of our major achievements was passing fair-credit legislation that enabled women to get credit in their own names.

When Jimmy Carter was president, I served on the Secretary's Advisory Committee on the Rights and Responsibilities of Women. I took a particular interest in pension and Social Security reform.

Why do you have mixed emotions about the progression of the women's movement?
A lot of the things for which I've stood have almost become muted because some younger women haven't really learned the pain and struggle of women in the '60s and '70s who sacrificed time and effort to try to promote women's issues.

Maybe we're a victim of our own success. I don't see any visible presence of some of the old-fashioned women's organizations. Many women now in the labor market don't have as much time as we had for civic effort. We got our independence and now we have to economically support ourselves.

When I was working the precincts, women would say they had to talk to their husbands before supporting a candidate. Many women now say they always vote for women, so we think we've made a big switch. But, no, we shouldn't vote for a candidate simply because she's a woman. We should vote for the best candidate.

But you don't often think the best candidate is a Republican woman?
It was easy for me to work with many of the Republican women involved in the Women's Political Caucus because we had the same goals. I don't see many moderate Republican women anymore in Congress.

Serving as president of the Metropolitan Housing Coalition and the Coalition for the Homeless gave you a unique perspective of one of society's most serious problems.
The homeless picture in Louisville used to focus on men who had a problem with alcoholism and lived in flophouses or boarding rooms. As the economic situation changed, the nature of homelessness changed to families.

How have you not been overwhelmed by the scope of problems with which you have dealt?
Piece by piece, I've been able to effect change, either by myself or with other folks. I never give up.

What's the biggest risk you've ever taken?
Being upfront about women's issues, particularly the issue of abortion and women being able to maintain their own identity and make their own choices. When I jumped into the women's movement, "women's libber" was a disparaging label. I was always proud to wear it.

What's the most important thing you've learned in life?
To keep my mouth shut at times. I think I've toned down my rhetoric.

Is there anything that intimidates you?
No. I've been a fighter all my life. An employee once told me about myself, "People either love you or hate you." That's the way life is. Sometimes when you're out there, people disagree you with you. If I believe in something strongly, it's okay if I'm not liked.

How do you feel about aging?
It's difficult. I've been a self assertive woman---I hope not in an obnoxious way. To be treated differently now that I'm older takes a lot of patience and tolerance. When I'm called Sweetie at the grocery store, even though I know the person is well meaning, I think, "Lady, I've never been a Sweetie". What's interesting is that it's often other women who speak to me that way.

Selam Deneke

Your life growing up in Ethiopia was centered on your family, wasn't it?

My mother was always very loving and caring. My father passed away when I was 15 years old. Our house was always the gathering spot for our extended family. I had many cousins who would spend time with my five brothers, five sisters, and me. All I knew was having fun.

Coming to live in the United States wasn't part of your original plan.

I was a French teacher and was hoping for a scholarship to go to France. My sister invited me to come here for a visit, and I decided to live here. But I didn't give up teaching. I studied early childhood education and taught at Jefferson Community College and at Bright Horizons. I was very happy teaching because I wanted to give children love and to be a role model.

Your attempt at being a matchmaker was a failure that turned into a huge success!

When I first met the person who's now my husband, I tried to fix him up with my cousin. I'm so glad that didn't work out.

How did you get into the restaurant business?

My husband said I was a great cook and should make money at it. He owned Abyssinia restaurant. He was the chef, bartender, everything. I joined him in the business. We eventually moved the restaurant a couple of times, and it's become very successful.

But you had to change the name of the restaurant from Abyssinia to Queen of Sheba because so many people couldn't pronounce it? You must have thought we were idiots.

Well, it was kind of shocking. And at first, Louisvillians didn't understand Ethiopian food, which was discouraging. But as we taught them about the food, they became very receptive. Louisvillians are very laid-back, beautiful people, and they have been wonderful to us. We now feel so at home here.

Cooking is much more than simply a business to you.

The body needs to be nurtured with quality food. I enjoy cooking and making people happy. I learned to cook from my mother. I share her love of entertaining, of sharing meals with friends and family.

Your restaurant has plenty of meat dishes on the menu, but aren't you primarily a vegetarian?

Mostly I'm a vegetarian, but I do eat meat. I grew up eating lots of vegetables but wasn't completely removed from meat. I watched my father and brother slaughter the cows and goats. I wanted to be strong and show that I could compete with the men, so I tried to help by taking off the skin. It didn't bother me. But it was a man's world and they really didn't want me to help. They told me just to have fun.

Do you still think it's a man's world?

Yes! Why do men always get the better jobs and have an easier life? I think there are many more pressures on women than on men. It seems that women are responsible for everything, certainly raising the children. Men don't want to put their mind to it and to be involved as much as they should. My husband helps, but not as much as I'd like. I look at him and think, "I'm doing it and you can, too."

How do you like to spend your spare time?

I'm a yogi. I get up early so I have time to practice my yoga. I also like to have fun with my friends and family, maybe going to movies or playing sports.

What traits do you most like in a person?

A sense of humor and intelligence.

And least?

Ignorance and having no interest in understanding other people and the world.

Who's the most fascinating woman you know?

My mom. She's my role model. She helped me to become centered, to be myself, and never pushed me to follow in her footsteps.

What's your biggest regret?

That I didn't spend much time with my father before he passed away. I was young and wanted to live a different part of my life.

What do you like best about yourself?

I enjoy life.

And least?

God made me beautifully. I don't want to complain. I might like to be a little skinnier, but it's not a big issue. I'm complete.

Vicki Dortch

You're now a news anchor at WLKY. Why did you choose broadcast journalism as a career?
I fell in love with the cameras and lights while taking a radio and television course at Murray State. I minored in journalism. One of my first jobs was at the NBC affiliate in Paducah. I did a little of everything from reporting to editing. I came to WLKY thinking it would be for two years. It's now been 23 years. I love it because every day is different. I'm not relinquishing that news desk to anyone!

How do you separate yourself from the story?
It's very difficult. I often wish I could tell the viewers what I really think in a commentary, but they're not watching to hear what I think. Those of us at the station joke that people would be surprised to see our reactions to stories during commercial breaks. Ninety percent of the viewers would probably agree with our opinions.

What was the most difficult story you've covered?
A missing child. Everyone, including our crew, was searching for her. I asked the mother every question other than, "Did you kill your daughter?" But at the time I wouldn't have asked that. Now that I have less faith in mankind, I might ask that question if I were in the same situation. One morning she admitted she threw her daughter off the bridge. I was so emotionally invested in the story. Children's stories usually get to me. They probably affect viewers the same way.

What has been the biggest challenge in your life?
Being a divorced mom, although I think of myself as a single mom. Many times I feel like I'm not giving 100 percent to my child and 100 percent to my work. I'm very close to my son. The years have gone by too quickly. I'm not ready to become an empty nester.

And the biggest accomplishment?
Personally it would be raising my son. Professionally it would be making WLKY the number one station in the market. When I started, we were in third place. We always felt as if we were behind just because we were WLKY. WHAS would get the stories and the breaks. My colleagues and I have worked hard. It's been a team effort, not one specific reporter or anchor. I'm so proud of it. We don't brag about ourselves enough.

Are you friends with anchors at other stations?
We have a very friendly competition.

Can you ever let loose and be yourself in public?
The best way to go to the grocery is wearing sunglasses and a ball cap and with no make-up. I can go anywhere and be myself. Some days it's just Vicki Dortch looking bad. It's nice to be recognized because that means people are watching. But, truthfully, many people tell me they recognize my voice. When they're listening to the television news, they may not even be looking at me as they cook dinner or get ready for bed.

What's the most important thing you've learned about yourself?
That I'm resilient and stronger than I thought. I can do it on my own.

Whom would you most want to interview?
It would have been Jackie O. I would have wanted to go back to the day President Kennedy was shot and relive it from her perspective. Now I'd like to interview Hillary Clinton, not about Bill and not about Monica Lewinsky, but about her own aspirations. It looks like her job has taken its toll on her. I'd also like to interview Casey Anthony if she would tell me the truth.

If you weren't on television, what would you be doing?
I'd love to be a singer but I can't sing. I'd love to be a model but I'm not tall enough. Really, I can't imagine having any occupation other than a news anchor. This is my dream job.

Is there anything you'd change about yourself if you could?
I'd like to have thick hair. I'd like to be 5'8" or 5'9" instead of 5'6" and to be able to eat anything I wanted and still wear a size 2.

Do you have a major regret?
Marrying the person I married.

What trait do you most like in a person?
Loyalty.

What's next for you?
The world is open, isn't it? I haven't mapped out a plan. Maybe I need one.

Kathy Drane

You had a life-changing experience leading up to your founding Hopeful Hearts, an organization that provides medical and nutrition aid and basic necessities to orphan children in developing and/or Third-World countries.
My husband had been involved in mission work in Ukraine. My daughter and I accompanied him on a vacation there to see the work he had been doing in an orphanage. The children were tied to old metal beds in a room with no lights. They had little medication. Although it was heartbreaking, I didn't feel like the work was for me and wanted to go home. On our last day, our 12-year-old daughter spotted identical twin girls. I sat on the curb and held them. They were precious but I was almost 47 years old and had no desire for other children. My daughter started sobbing and asked, "Why is your heart so hard? We have such a big house for just three people." I eventually put the little girls down and we left the orphanage. We came home to our normal lives. About a month later I asked if my daughter and husband wanted to look into what it would take to adopt the girls. Ukraine had been open for adoption for only two months. The adoption process was complicated and laborious but, finally, we were approved to adopt the girls. But by that time, Natasha, one of the twins, had died from a respiratory infection.

When I went back to adopt Olla, she was 2 ½ years old but weighed only 16 pounds. She would eat all the food I would take her each visit, but she wouldn't talk or make eye contact with me. I had decided to leave in a couple of days if she didn't react or respond because I didn't think I could deal with special needs. That night I cried until I couldn't catch my breath. I railed at God and I prayed. The next afternoon I opened the door to her room. She had her back to me. I passed out the treats and saw that she had stood up. I held out my hand to her. She began to run toward me a little, laced her hands in mine, looked at me and said, "Mamma." I stayed and got to know her and grew to know God in a way I had not known him before. We adopted Olla and brought her home. The Southeast Outlook newspaper wrote an article about our experience. We received calls from all over the United States asking for our guidance to help other parents adopt from Ukraine. Over the past 14 years, I have developed a staff in Ukraine. Hopeful Hearts has placed six hundred children. We also support children's homes in Ukraine, Sri Lanka, Myanmar and Indonesia. We take in children who live in slums or are abandoned in the streets. We increase their diet and provide medicine and clothing. In Ukraine, we have also started transitional living homes for children who graduate out of the orphanage system. I feel this has been my calling.

What has been the biggest challenge of your life?
Deciding to take what I feel l like was a leap of faith into the adoption and this ministry. It's a huge undertaking to commit to so many people throughout the world. People are counting on us. I'm a very fortunate woman and have been blessed. I have had every opportunity and have been given every advantage. I married a wonderful man and have a fantastic birth daughter. And I can't imagine having gone through my life without Olla.

What's the most important thing you've learned about yourself?
That I can do it; that I can make a difference. It's a matter of having perseverance and setting my mind to it. Also, when I was younger, I tried to be someone I wasn't. But over the years I have figured out that's tiresome.

Other than the people in your life, what couldn't you live without?
My faith.

Do you have any advice for young women?
Make the most of who you are; don't try to be someone you're not. There's so much more to life than trying to impress people you don't even know. Find something to do with your life.

Is there anything you would change about yourself?
I would like to be able to sing. And I wish I were a bit more detail-oriented, more organized, and thinner. But, there is nothing major I would change.

Summer Eliason

You're a jewelry designer and an interior designer. So, you're able to express yourself through a variety of ways.

They're disciplines that have their similarities and differences, but they're both very much focused on color and texture, and finding the right fit for the individual. And they both have a lot of personality. My work allows me to express myself and lets my clients express themselves. I'm fortunate to be able to do something I enjoy so much.

What inspires your designs?

Traveling provides wonderful inspiration both for interiors and for jewelry. When I design jewelry, I design it as if I'm going to wear it. I love and would wear everything I design. My jewelry is fun, colorful, and a little eclectic. Some pieces are large statement necklaces. They're not dainty. They can definitely make an outfit. Color is equally important in my interior designs, as can be seen by the color I have going on in my own home.

Your career as a designer didn't follow a straight and narrow path.

No, my stepfather kind of pushed me toward architecture, but I knew it wasn't for me. I was always interested in art and received my B.S. in design studies from the School of Architecture at the University of Colorado. I worked for an interior designer in Telluride. The store closed for a few months when the ski season ended. During that time I worked for a store in town that sold furniture, jewelry, most everything. I had no interest in jewelry but the owner made me learn how it was made. The next thing I knew I was using all my paycheck to buy stones. I soon started selling to stores and galleries. That was the beginning of my designing jewelry. When I decided I didn't want to stay in Colorado, I moved to Louisville. My father invited me to work at Jenkins Eliason Interiors. I love working in interior design, but my real love is jewelry.

You've had some interesting and unique travel adventures!

I spent a Semester at Sea while I was in college. We went to fabulous places such as Brazil, Cuba, Malaysia, Vietnam, China, Japan, and India. We even went on safari in Tanzania. One of my favorite countries to visit was Cuba. We were the first group of students allowed to go there after the ban on travel was lifted. I was amazed to see how it was kind of stuck in time. I was very interested to visit China because I had studied the Forbidden City and wanted to experience it in person. And I'll never forget how massive and impressive Shanghai appeared. I have to admit that I was a bit scared in India. I freaked out. We were sort of

dropped off in the country, letting us do whatever we wanted for a couple of days. There couldn't be a culture more different than ours. Semi trucks and cows were all on the road together. I thought if anything was going to happen to me, it would happen there. Once I became comfortable going out and doing things, the time in India was a great experience.

I also completed an architecture study abroad program in Rome. I loved the city and traveling around the country.

How do you spend your time when you're not designing?

I like to work out, run, bike, travel, and cook. I enjoy experimenting in the kitchen and entertaining.

What do you like best about yourself?

I have a lot of interests and I'm creative. I'm good at problem-solving and can usually make things work.

And least?

I'm not as patient as I'd like to be. When I make a decision, I'm ready to go, but sometimes I think it would be better to take a step back. On the other hand, I think my husband takes too long to make a decision. Maybe there's a good middle ground.

What's the best decision you have ever made?

Coming back to Louisville. Or maybe marrying my husband. He was my high school sweetheart. We were separated for years and got back together.

Annette Ellard

Your mission has become working with refugees from Burma. How did that happen?

About 10 years ago we went on a mission to northern Thailand. We were to paint a Karen youth hostel where students beyond the sixth grade go to school. Some in our group noticed that my husband Steve and I were doing a better job of bridging the cultural and language barriers than we were painting. They suggested that we should talk and they should paint. We soon knew that our lives were going to change but we didn't know how drastically they would change.

As videographers, you became even more familiar with the refugees and their plight.

Burma has had the longest-running civil war in the world for more than 60 years. The Karen people are the largest of the ethnic minority groups and have maintained the fight against the Burmese government longer than any other group. We had produced a video for the Cooperative Baptist Fellowship that showed the efforts being undertaken to assist the Karen who were seriously underserved medically. What I remember most at the clinic are the children who suffered so severely from ear infections that they had developed hearing loss. Because of a lack of equipment, the doctor had to diagnose their ear infections by the smell of the children's ears. We also videotaped clinic visitations as well as training sessions that were held for leaders in the community. One of the leaders who came for training was so dedicated that he walked for three days to arrive at the clinic.

How did you become involved in helping the refugees resettle in Louisville?

We had a four-month education in refugee issues and the process of resettlement in the United States. We found out that Karen refugees were going to be resettled here because of political persecution. We thought there would be a few refugees but had no idea of the magnitude of the resettlement. Approximately 700 to 800 refugees from Burma have resettled in Louisville. Steve and I became the local experts on Karen people due to our previous experience with them. The Karen people say that they feel as if they are newborns in the United States. They look to us as parents to help them and show them the way to live as Americans. It's a huge honor and responsibility. We decided that our primary concern would be to meet their spiritual needs. We pray and worship with them in their homes and in church. We celebrate the big events in their lives, such as births, birthdays, and weddings.

We also help them get to medical appointments and to deal with social services. The day-to-day ministry is a mixed bag of pastoral care, social work, crisis management, and advocacy.

You've developed an intensely personal relationship with many of the Karen.

Our relationships with them are very dear to us. They have made us one of them. On the first Mother's Day after the Karen had become part of our congregation, the Karen leader said to me, "Welcome, Karen Mother. Your children have been waiting for you." They call Steve and me Karen Father and Mother. The wedding of one of our Karen daughters had special significance to us. Steve walked her down the aisle. She asked me to give the sermon. It was the coolest thing I've ever done.

What's the best decision you ever made?

Marrying Steve, because he and I share the same passions. I never dreamed that my life could be so good. I knew early on that God wanted to give me children in a different way. I didn't know what that would be. I thought maybe I would adopt older children. Now I have 500 children.

What do you hope for the future?

To have the opportunity to live and work with the Karen people in their real home, not in a resettlement situation. The hardest thing for me to see is that, as many good things as the Karen people have here in America, they want to be in their own country. My dream is that. I never stop being touched by the comment of a Karen friend who loves the flowers and trees she sees in Louisville. She always says, "When my country gets democracy, you and I will take them and plant them in Burma."

Christine Fellingham

You brought your fashion and beauty journalism experience from New York to Louisville and are now Fashion Editor of *The Courier-Journal* and Editor-in-chief of *Her Scene*. While you were in New York, you had a bit of a *Devil Wears Prada* experience.

My first job out of college was as a roving assistant with Condé Nast. I worked at *GQ* and, for a time, got stuck at *Brides*, which was a total snooze. While at *Vogue*, I did research for Shirley Lord, who was the beauty director. I spent about five days Xeroxing her little black book, but I also got to do some reporting and writing. Anna Wintour was already hitting her stride. She would slink around the office in her sunglasses and people would quake. Shirley wanted me to interview with Anna. I was told I had to have a total makeover just to get the appointment. I didn't want *Vogue* that badly. It was interesting to see what some girls would do just to work at the magazine. There was a lot of getting people lunch and sectioning grapefruit and having to lay it out in certain directions, if you can believe it. But there's no place better to be than at *Vogue* for someone who wants to work in fashion.

"Intoxicating and interesting" was how you described your position as Beauty Editor at *Glamour* magazine.

After I left *Vogue*, I worked at *Glamour*, eventually moving up to Beauty Editor. I was amazed at how much actual business is involved in covering fashion and beauty, and how much power I came in contact with. I spent a lot of time reporting, but my job also included having fancy lunches with CEOs of huge companies and riding around town in limousines. That's just what it was about.

Then there was Oprah!

I was offered the really big position as Beauty Editor of *O, The Oprah Magazine*. It was such a great opportunity I couldn't refuse. I didn't sleep for the first four months because of the stress of developing a prototype for the magazine. Oprah is a very nice person but also a perfectionist. Talk about driven. She works all the time. She's fair but extremely blunt. She and I got along really well, and she was very complimentary of my beauty coverage.

Was moving back to Louisville a culture shock?

Well, yes. My husband and I had started a family in New York but thought we might like to raise the children somewhere else. We're both from Louisville. I had been receiving postcards from the Louisville Chamber of Commerce that were designed to lure people back. My husband and I took a test to help determine which city would be best for us. It was Louisville. We picked up and

came back. I stayed on as Contributing Editor of Oprah's magazine, as well as for *Glamour* and *Good Housekeeping*. I didn't quickly acclimate to how mothers dressed around Louisville. One day it was suggested that I not wear heels to the playground. My wardrobe seemed out of place for my reading and mommy groups because I had always worn black in New York and the moms here were in colors. Another adjustment was slowing down how I talked and acted. I soon understood that rushing is considered rude here. I had to work at being more patient and doings things at a different pace. I was thrilled to see that Louisville women take fantastic care of themselves and are very interested in fashion. And I couldn't believe that Louisville has such great clothing stores. All of that, and the city's lack of a fashion magazine, led me to approach *The Courier-Journal* about starting one.

Are you a shopaholic?

Although I love fashion and enjoy the aesthetics, I'm not an idle shopper. I'm very mission-oriented.

What haven't you done that you would like to do?

I always wanted to be a magazine editor, be happily married, and be a mother, and I have. Being able to launch *Her Scene* was much more exciting than being beauty editor of Oprah's magazine. How many people get to start a magazine from scratch? I've been so lucky.

How do you feel about aging?

I think it's a shame we're not allowed to age anymore. We have wonderful choices of surgeries and procedures, but I think we've gone down the slippery slope. The value of youth over all else drives me crazy. In chasing youth, we devalue the things we've accomplished. I hate to see that we herald 21 year olds who haven't done anything.

What would people be surprised to know about you?

That I have been known to tape my hem.

C. J. Fletcher

You have said you will always be a painter. Do you have periods during which you feel a total lack of creativity and have nothing to express?

I used to have periods when I didn't know what I wanted to paint next. I knew I had to reach a certain point in my art career where I wasn't just painting something that I liked but to paint something universal that all people could relate to. My series "The Doors" is about the doors we enter and exit each day. Every day each one of us goes through some type of a doorway, and we must be conscious of the rewards, consequences, and retribution behind each door.

You also say a painting is never finished until you can feel it in your soul. What do you mean?

That's when you can look at your painting with a smile and say, "I'm done." Sometimes if you continue to work a painting you can ruin it. One time I was so frustrated with a painting that I slammed it against the wall, stepped on it, slammed it again, and threw it out the back door. That's how frustrating art can be when you're trying to please someone else and not the inner soul.

In what ways are artists different from the rest of us?

I truly believe artists are no different from anyone else. I believe we were all put here on earth with some kind of artistic talent, with some people accidentally stumbling on it, some seeking it, and some determined to make it happen. It may not be the talent you want, but the one you have to settle for. I always wanted to be a singer but survived only one year in the Women's Day Choir when I was told to go back to painting.

What has been the most defining moment in your life?

When a person invited her friends to an art show for me in her home. I had a body of work built up but didn't know how to get it on the market. I took 19 of my paintings and sold 18 of them. I'll always be grateful that she took the time to get me started.

And your major disappointment?

That in my early years I didn't know what life was all about and how you had to prepare yourself for the days to come.

Other than the people in your life, what couldn't you live without?

I can't imagine what my life would be like without the talent that God gave me. I love to paint. It relaxes me. It's such a joy to be able to create something that brings joy to others.

What's the biggest risk you've ever taken?

Jumping off the diving board in Algonquin Park into 12 feet of water knowing that I couldn't swim. My mom had paid for swimming lessons but I could never get the hang of it. On graduation day I wanted to prove that if I dove off the board, I would instantly learn to swim. The guard had to rescue me.

Do you have any regrets?

My regrets could be my downfall, so I don't dwell on them. Who knows what roads you must travel and what "doors" you must open and close before life becomes what it's supposed to be? We can never go back and change what we have done, but we can be grateful for what we have now. We should never stay stuck on regret.

Is there anything about yourself that you'd change if you could?

I'd be able to sing.

What's the most important lesson you have learned?

When you're in a meeting and someone asks for suggestions, keep your mouth shut because your suggestion will become a project you'll be appointed to. But, that's okay for me because I like innovative things to do.

Finish the sentence, "I wish women would…

continue to stand up for their rights and prove to the world that we're just as important as men." I have always been a tomboy and still feel that I can do any job that a man can do and, if truly tested, I can do it even better.

How do you measure success?

By the progress and accomplishments I have made in my life and the impact I have had on others.

How do you feel about aging?

I don't mind it at all. I always liked the gray look around the temples, which I seem to be getting. I try my best to stay away from doctors. They seem to want to give you preventive medicine that ends up harming you.

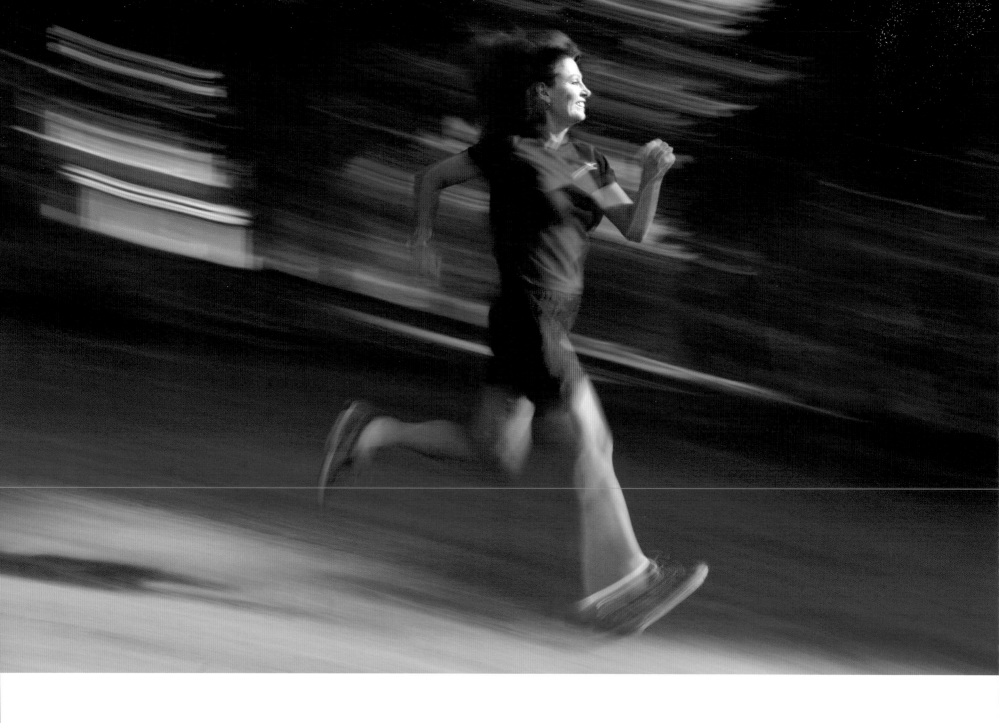

Jill Force

You're an attorney and have worked in several corporations. Have you ever felt there was a glass ceiling?

The view of the role of women in the workplace has evolved dramatically since I moved to Louisville in the mid-1970s. At that time, there were very few of us and we were viewed as anomalies. Yes, I was asked to get coffee, and yes, I didn't get access to some opportunities early on because of my sex. Some people were overly hostile and others were bewildered by my presence. Over time, that resistance has faded. I have had access to many situations, particularly board seats, because male coworkers promoted me. On the other hand, I don't think anyone believes that it's a perfect world out there. At times it's just harder for a woman's voice to be heard.

Do you think you have had to be better and more aggressive than your male counterparts?

That's a complicated question. Yes and no. Sometimes women are more visible and that visibility can work for or against you.

What effect, if any, did the women's movement have on you?

It had a powerful and formative effect on me. Absent the efforts of the women in the '60s and '70s that raised my awareness of self-imposed and societal limitations, my life might have taken a very different course. I am forever grateful to those pioneers.

In three or four words, how would you describe yourself?

Energetic, driven, focused, fun.

What has been the biggest challenge in your life?

Finding the right tradeoff between my role as a mother and as a professional. I wouldn't have it any other way. I love both roles, and I think I'm a better mother and a better professional because I do both, but that doesn't make it easy. Nothing that rewarding is easy, though.

What has been your major disappointment?

I try not to look back.

Other than the people in your life, what couldn't you live without?

My running shoes.

What haven't you done that you would like to do?

Travel. Get my golf handicap under 15. Read more of the world's great books.

Is there anything people would be surprised to know about you?

I'm the oldest of eight kids. The Force kids were a pack, and we were tough.

Who's the most fascinating woman you know or know about?

I think Hillary Clinton is terrific. She's complicated and smart and just keeps going.

What trait do you most like in a person?

Kindness.

And least?

Hypocrisy.

What would you change about yourself if you could?

I would be taller the next time around.

How do you feel about aging?

It's great to have the confidence that comes with decades of experience. But that's about the only good thing about aging.

What's next for you?

I need to get to the office.

Laura Frazier

You're one of the most well-known people in Louisville. Is that fun or is it a burden?

It can be both. I'm a private person, so it can be a burden because of the lack of privacy. I'd rather be known by my first name than last name, and who I am, not who my father was. It didn't hit me until after college, when I got jobs where I realized there were people who wanted to be friends with me for the wrong reasons. I still worry about that. I like to escape to my home out West because there I'm just Laura. I have a lot of fun there because no one has an agenda.

You are associated with many organizations and are so active in the community. Does that just come naturally?

Part of my father's philosophy, which I share, was to be out of the office 30 percent of the time. It's very important to be part of the community and to do things. I have been involved with the Kentucky Derby Museum since the early 1990s. I'm on a lot of boards. Helping to support Dr. Suzanne Ildstad's bone marrow stem cell transplantation research has been my real mission for a while.

You had a life-threatening illness.

I had colon cancer in 2001. I'm happy to be here but it changes your perspective. It's to die for, but I'm trying to change it to "It's to live for" because if you die, you can't have it again. I think you have to find the humor in stuff. I participated in a clinical trial. I never knew if I received the placebo or the real drug. Occasionally they'd call and ask if I was alive. They definitely lacked a bedside manner. But the whole experience gave me a new respect for life and for people going through these things.

Do you worry about dying?

I don't contemplate it that much. But I have a colonoscopy every year. I think of it as defensive driving.

Perhaps one of the most frequent questions asked of philosophers and theologians is, "Why do bad things happen to good people?" How would you answer that?

To give them the inner strength to deal with the experience, learn from the experience, and then grow into a better person from the experience.

What do you like to do when you're not busy with nonprofit work or in your role as chairman of Bittners?

I paint and do mosaics. And I have tiled all my bathrooms myself. I also like to cook and experiment with new recipes. In the world I live in, I can be half business and half creative. Bittners has been a great outlet for both.

At Bittners you're surrounded by the best of the best in home design. And your own home must be one of the most spectacular in Louisville. Inviting you over for dinner sounds slightly scary.

No! People who know me don't think that at all. I love to see what other people have done in their homes. It's kind of like opening a Christmas present.

Other than the people in your life, what couldn't you live without?

My artwork and things I have made and designed.

What's the most important thing you have learned about yourself?

That I have no patience. I'm trying to get better about that. My kids would say I have totally mellowed. A lot of that is because of the cancer and knowing that there is so much you can't control—the white count, the hair falling out. I'm probably a nicer person now and I don't get rattled like I used to.

What's the biggest risk you've ever taken?

Going to work for my father even though I did write the book on being a Daddy's girl.

Is there anything people would be surprised to know about you?

If I don't know someone well, I'm kind of quiet. So they might be surprised that I have a sense of humor. And I can tell some very funny stories.

What do you like best about yourself?

The ability to laugh at myself.

And least?

My lack of ability to let go and let someone else be in control of me and/or my fate.

If you could be anywhere in the world right now, where would you be and what would you be doing?

In Park City, Utah at Deer Valley on a sunny day first thing in the morning. At the top of Magnet taking a deep breath before taking that first turn, followed by the second turn…

Sarah Fritschner

You were the food editor for *The Courier-Journal*, are now coordinator of the Louisville Farm to Table project, and are the editor of *edibleLOUISVILLE*. Was writing about or being involved with food always your goal?
I liked horses but it became clear that to break into any kind of horse business required money and resources. So I went for food and majored in nutrition. I wanted to save the world with Vitamin A. I became fascinated that health and well-being are so dependent on what you eat. I thought, "Golly, it's so easy to improve people's health." I found that it's not so easy. It's hard for people to change their habits.

You take a user-friendly, nondictatorial approach to people and food.
I approach food with more joy than dogma, I hope. People are getting the message; they're learning that the right food can make them well, and the right food can help them live well. There's a whole lot of good food. Some people might think a Blizzard is good, and it is, but ripe strawberries are also good, so why not choose something that's good for you and tastes good too?

Why are some people so resistant to cooking healthy foods at home?
There's more to cooking than cooking. There's thinking, planning, shopping, cooking, setting the table, cleaning up, and throwing out food if it goes bad. Some people don't care what's for dinner. Some may wonder why they should make any of these choices. I sympathize with people who struggle to get dinner on the table.

My interest in local food has always been that it's more appealing than something that has been flown in from California. You don't get to eat local strawberries often but they taste 100 percent better than the gross California ones. I've noticed my own children would choose a local apple over junk food because it tasted better. I don't mean that they would never choose junk food. Most people do every once in a while.

Your new job is about education.
Less than one percent of food will be purchased at a farmers' market. My job is to include local food at schools, restaurants, or workplace cafeterias—places that probably don't purchase food from farmers' markets. It's all part of the Farm to Table project.

What haven't you done that you would like to do?
I haven't saved the world. I'm not adventurous, not someone who wants to go to Paris and eat foie gras. I want to help make Kentucky agriculture a success. It's fun and exhilarating for me. I love working with farmers and fresh food. I love helping figure out how to get a farmer turned from growing tobacco, which is failing, to growing something that will provide him another income.

What's the best decision you ever made?
Obviously, having children because they are life-changing, and marrying my husband. I'd been obsessed with horses all my life. I had a friend who had ovarian cancer who said, "Do me a favor. Get a horse." I thought, "I'm not getting any smarter, richer, or younger." So I bought a horse, Vicar Hines. He was named for the man who baptized my son. However, I didn't know the man who had owned him and I didn't know the horse. It was just a strange coincidence.

In the mid-1990s I was planning the Ohio Valley Harvest Festival, a food festival that paired restaurants with farmers and was set up on the Belvedere. Another food person who is well known in town came into the middle of the planning. She started rattling all the things that could wrong. It would have been in my nature to abandon the project at that point because of her criticism. She was sort of saying, "Who do you think you are?" and implying that it was too much for me do to. I couldn't not do it. I stuck it out and it changed me completely. It made me face a fear of failing. I understand that failure of some measure was not only okay, but common. It was a wonderful event for a few years. It was wild. I'm thankful that everything happened as it did.

What's your biggest regret?
I have no major regrets. I think we learn from our mistakes. But I might regret little things like when I reacted defensively. Would leaving *The Washington Post* be a regret? I met a man, had his children. I wasn't happy in Washington and didn't feel like I was doing important work. So I don't regret it.

Hope Crain Gardiner

Why do you say that some of life's most amazing adventures happen when you go with the flow?

After I graduated with a degree in horticulture, I traveled around the state certifying organic farms. They ranged from backyard gardens to 200 to 300-acre farms that grew everything from tomatoes to soy beans to beef. I drove through hollers and passed people who were sitting on their porches holding their shotguns. Visiting places such as Beyond Yonder and Hell for Certain, I met some unforgettable people. One of the most memorable was a woman, a real character, who grew ginseng and lived in a cabin in eastern Kentucky. I will always remember her telling me that before I arrived, she had removed the copperheads from her outhouse in case I needed to use it. She was extremely happy living a very austere life and was thrilled when she got glass windows for her cabin. On the property was a more modern house where she could have lived, but she was satisfied with her cabin. She had everything she wanted. Meeting people like her changed how I felt about my own life and put things in perspective for me. I really learned that it's not important to keep up with the Joneses and that sometimes the simplest things in life can be the most rewarding and fulfilling.

You and your husband are part of a family that has been in the nursery business for more than 100 years. You help run the business, cultivate a garden that would make Martha Stewart proud, and you raise chickens, goats, and pigs. But there's something about you that says "city girl."

I grew up in town with all the benefits of a city girl. I modeled while I was in high school, joined a sorority in college, and later became a member of the Junior League. I'm involved in a lot of civic activities and am on several boards. But when the day is over, I'm definitely a country girl at heart.

In your garden are potatoes, green beans, tomatoes, okra, watermelon, onions, carrots, lettuce, squash, pumpkins, eggplant, and many herbs. Do you laugh at shoppers who seem perfectly content to buy produce at the supermarket? Or do you feel sorry for them?

Neither, really. But I wish people weren't losing knowledge of how to provide food for themselves. And it's sad to see so many kids who don't have any idea from where their food comes. They think carrots just come in a plastic bag. It is also sad to watch the epidemic of urban sprawl and the disappearance of farm land.

What has been the biggest challenge in your life?

My grandmother fought cancer for 54 years. Not one day did she ever complain or feel sorry for herself. The major challenge in my life is continuing; it's to remember that we always have the choice to feel sorry for ourselves or to make the best of any situation. I try to keep a positive attitude and hope that I'm raising my children to look at life the same way.

Is there anything that intimidates you?

When people come across as very strong, my initial reaction might be intimidation. But I soon realize that I can learn from them. There are times when I wonder if I will be able to do a particular thing. I might be intimidated at first, but then I become determined to do it. I used to be afraid of heights, so I decided to parachute and jump out of an airplane. Whenever I'm told I can't do something, I'll find a way to do it.

Other than the people in your life, what couldn't you live without?

A hot shower and a Pepsi in the morning.

About what do you most worry?

Like any parent, I worry about my kids, not only on a day-to-day basis, but in terms of what the world's going to be like when they grow up. I worry about the big picture. I think that's okay. I know my parents still worry about me.

What would people be surprised to know about you?

That I'm not afraid to get dirty and to do hard, physical work. They'd probably also be surprised that I'm a pretty good shot. My dad used to take me duck hunting. I'm as comfortable with a shotgun as I am in a ball gown.

Dawne Gee

As a news anchor at WAVE 3, you're one of the most public figures in Louisville. Do you feel as if you always have to be on guard when you're out in public?

I don't care. That may not be the smartest thing. Early in my career, my father said, "Seriously, you're not going out like that!" I was dressed very casually and wasn't wearing makeup. I told him, "You know what? They probably won't look any better than I do, so why should I have to walk around all made up?" I'm just not going to worry about that when I'm not on the air. All day long people tell me I look prettier in person, and that I don't look as fat as I do on television. I'm not sure how to take that. Mostly everyone I meet is wonderful and very kind to me. I enjoy and appreciate every kiss I get at the grocery and every hug at the gas station.

You have degrees in communication and biology. Now that you're in communication, the big question is, "Why biology?"

Biology was easy for me. I thought about being a doctor, but my first observation of an autopsy was of a 10-year-old boy. That was enough for me. My heart wasn't strong enough to be a doctor. If I had pursued medicine, I would have had to write prescriptions for myself. My mother suggested I become a podiatrist. Really? There was no way I was going to mess with anyone's feet. I got a job as a pharmaceutical sales rep and made lots of money. I hated it and cried at the edge of my bed every day. I took a radio job, as news director for WRKA, earning $50,000 or $60,000 less. I thought my mother was going to kill me. But I knew money wasn't going to make me happy.

You were told you'd never make it on television.

I was bound and determined to work at WAVE. I applied nine times before they hired me, and then it was as a writer/producer. The news director said I needed to get a realistic dream, that I would never be a success on air. Finally I was allowed to fill in for someone who was on air. It went very well. When her contract ended, I was offered the job. In my head, I kept thinking, "For all you folks who said I couldn't do it, look at me now."

Isn't it difficult to hide your emotions when covering tragic stories?

I'm not sure I do hide it well. When I was new to the job, I cried, and still do. I've never become used to it, but I have learned to tuck it away in what I call my prayer place. You may hear me say on the air that I will pray for a family involved in such a story. I don't understand why people do what we do to each other. I hope I never understand.

Somehow you're able to laugh about your very serious health problems.

My family always jokes about our struggles. It's how we deal with things. I've had lupus. I've had a breast tumor, a tumor on my uterus, and a brain tumor. I joke that I can't grow anything but tumors.

Whenever there's a fundraiser or community event, you seem to be there.

Because of my own health problems, I've often needed a hug and for someone to say it's going to be okay. I want to help other people with their problems. If I'm asked to help out with a fundraiser or some type of event, I'll do it as long as my schedule is clear. My kids started attending these events when they were young. They helped me bag groceries for the disabled, fed residents at Wayside Christian Mission on Thanksgiving, and walked with me for the American Cancer Society. I'm so happy that they're also now doing those things on their own, because they learned something and want to contribute.

What would people be surprised to know about you?

I love horror movies. I can't go to bed without having a horror movie on. My six-year-old grandson loves them, to. Can that be genetic?

Do you have aspirations beyond local television?

No. I was born and raised here. I would never leave my family. Well, maybe if someone offered me $20 million a year, I might slip out for a year! Seriously, life is too short. You only get one life, and if you live it right, that's all you need.

Marissa Ghavami

When did you know you wanted to be a singer and actor?

My mom said she couldn't get me to fall asleep unless she was dancing with me in her arms to VH1. I'd watch *The Wizard of Oz* and perform all the parts when I was three years old. I have tapes of me singing and dancing and doing monologues from *Bye Bye Birdie* when I was five.

Now you're an actor in New York, but your love of acting was nurtured at Louisville's Walden Theatre.

Walden was one of the dearest experiences of my life. There I was trained in Shakespeare, the Alexander technique, improv, stage combat—everything.

Living in L.A. and studying acting must have been exciting and daunting when you were only 15 years old.

It's hard to find a great acting class in Los Angeles. There's a mentality of a quick fix, and attending workshops. It took me a while to find a class I liked. But it was nothing compared to what I'm doing in New York.

So, New York is where you're really discovering yourself?

I'm studying singing and acting and am learning the old adage of the more I learn the more I realize the less I know. If you really set out to master your craft, you learn until the day you die. I will never think I've arrived. That wouldn't be fun because part of the fun is learning new things. That's what I love about the arts; they're not a mathematical equation. They're a mystery. It's a journey to find out more about your humanity and who you are.

How do you separate yourself from your character?

I'm of the school of thought that I'm against emotional memory. If for a part I have to be sobbing because my mother died, I'm not going to think about when my grandfather died because that's not healthy. I believe that isn't so much acting as getting really upset. I guess it does the trick but I think it's important to be a healthy, stable person as an artist. I study the Meisner technique; it's a series of exercises. The most basic thing is repetition. It's used to act truthfully under imaginary circumstances.

Do you prefer acting in comedy or drama?

I like to challenge myself to do everything. It feeds the same hunger inside of me, whether singing opera, playing the guitar, acting in a tragic Shakespearean play, or doing a sitcom. I don't prefer one over the other. I prefer good material.

Actors often have big egos. Do you?

I hope not. Acting shouldn't be about that. Actors who are in it for the right reason are often very humble and gracious. Sometimes actors come across very egoistical when actually they're very insecure.

It must have been unnervingly exciting to perform on NBC's *Showtime at the Apollo*.

That started the ball rolling for a real career outside Louisville when I was about 12. I had been sick in bed but my voice teacher said it was too late to back out. I was freaking and very nervous. The woman before me got booed off. I was terrified. At the end of the song, I looked up to the highest mezzanine level and saw two women who mouthed, "We love you." That opened up the possibility of pursuing my dream on a higher level.

You appeared on television in *Without a Trace*. Exciting or terrifying?

I wasn't nervous; I was just taking it all in. People's mikes were underneath their clothing so they spoke very softly. I wasn't used to that. The outside stimulation of not having experienced something like that before took a lot of energy out of me although it was only an eight-hour day.

Then on to the big screen!

I just finished a movie written by David Chase, who created *The Sopranos*. It's his first feature film. We shot for seven weeks in New York. David was the nicest, coolest man, kindest man.

Surviving auditions and waiting to hear the results must be grueling.

I try not to get too attached to parts because I'm a baby in this game. But it's hard when you're brought back in, perhaps again and again. It's a constant waiting game. This is a very vulnerable profession.

What's the most important thing you've learned about yourself?

That I'm stronger than I thought I was. And if you push yourself to certain limits, you'll surprise yourself with how much is inside of you and how much you can do. I've learned it's important to follow your dreams and desires and gut because we're meant to learn the things we learn along the path of chasing our dreams.

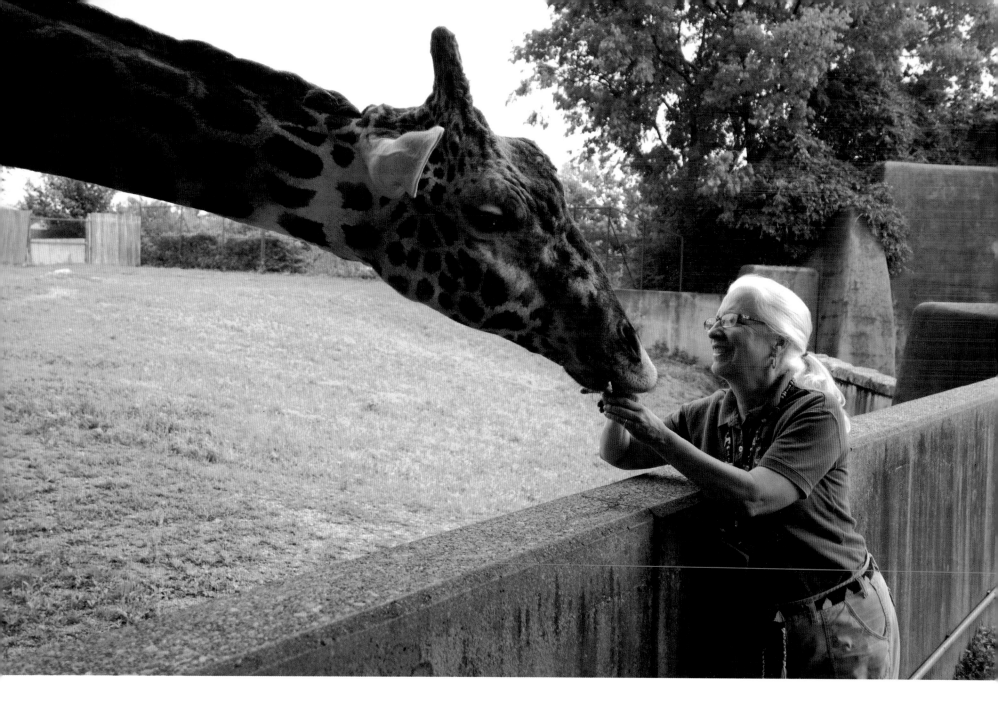

Marcelle T. Gianelloni

You grew up in Cuba. Why did you leave?
Castro took over the sugar company where my father worked. We moved to Miami thinking we would soon return to Cuba. That changed with the Bay of Pigs. Then we moved to New York where I became a real New Yorker.

As a lover of Russian literature, you were fortunate to experience life in Russia.
I saw an ad for "a mature young woman" to live with a diplomatic family in Moscow. I was a nanny for them and then got a job at the Anglo-American School of Moscow. It was a wonderful year. I've always loved Russian literature. I got to live it. On another occasion I opened a school for the United States consulate in Leningrad. It was the height of the Cold War. I was treated beautifully because I was an educator. I made some wonderful friends and did a little traveling although I wasn't permitted to leave the 25-mile radius without getting a visa. Finally I decided it was time to come back to the States.

How did you become involved with the Louisville Zoo?
I lived in New York until I met my husband, C. J. Pressma, who was from Louisville. He told me about Louisville's ballet, orchestra, and Actors Theatre. My heart brought me here. I began volunteering at the zoo and became hooked when a mother giraffe rejected her baby and I hand-fed him. I was also a science teacher at St. Francis and was involved in numerous environmental activities. When the job of Curator of Education at the zoo opened up, I applied and the rest is history. I combine my love for teaching with a sense of wonderment through a living classroom at the zoo. Our children today are totally disconnected from nature, so it's wonderful to observe how they respond to what they see and experience at the zoo. Becoming part of nature helps with creativity and concentration. Nature really is a healing place. I'm constantly thinking about how to create connections between people and ecosystems in order to foster feelings of caring and to inspire conservation action. Our mission at the zoo is to better the bond between people and the planet.

You've developed a special interest in crocodiles. How did that happen?
The Louisville Zoo has Cuban crocodiles, one of the most highly endangered crocodiles in the world. We work with other zoos and breed the crocodiles. Of course we realize that releasing them into their natural habitats is the ultimate objective, but we have to address the problems of poaching and unprotected habitats. Bill McMahan, also with the Louisville Zoo, and I went to Cuba to meet with biologists and educators. We set up a research project and education program at the Havana Zoo. It is a great project, but politics there, as all over the world, have a major impact on conservation. I'm continuing my work with the crocodiles through my position as Education Advisor for the Cuban Crocodile Species Survival Plan Committee.

One of your trips didn't go at all as you had planned.
I went to Colombia to learn about woolly monkeys. The people we were working with were held up by guerillas and we had to abandon camp.

What's the best decision you ever made?
Marrying my husband. I found my soul mate. Also, becoming an educator. That wasn't necessarily where I was going, but I love the feeling of inspiring people.

Looking to the future, what haven't you done that you would like to do?
My life has been a whirlwind. One thing has led to another. I'd like to do more conservation field work.

Who's the most fascinating woman you know or know about?
There are many. Certainly primatologist and anthropologist Jane Goodall, widely known for her study of wild chimpanzees in Tanzania. Also, I have so much admiration for a friend who works deep in the rain forest of Colombia. And I'm fortunate to have a lot of great women in my life. My friends are awesome.

What's your biggest regret?
I'm not in tune with regrets. I'm the type of person who moves on. Leaving Cuba at the age of 15 changed my life dramatically. I'm very critical of myself and am never completely satisfied with what I've done. But I'm a great believer in going on and figuring out solutions.

Magda Weck
Gonzalez

Some people refer to you as a psychic, but you correct them.

A psychic is seen as someone who reads the future. I read Tarot cards, but I also conduct ceremonies, teach, contact spirits, and heal, both hands–on and with herbs. I call myself a Shawomoon, not shaman. *Sha* means holy or blessed. *Man*, or male, is seen as a witch doctor or medicine man. But *wo* refers to female and working with the moon.

Early in my life I realized I had the talent to see and know things that other people couldn't. My grandmother taught me about spirits. She and her friends did table tapping and séances. They put their hands on a table and asked questions of the spirits. While my cat and I sat underneath, the table would rise and tap—two taps for no, three for yes.

You're pictured here with a sword and dagger.
What is their significance?

I see myself as a Warrior Woman, a protector, and a healer of animals and nature. When I go into a trance to contact the spirits, I sit with my sword across my lap and my dagger in my left hand. One of my cats sits beside me. The sword, dagger and cat help to connect me to my home as I walk the middle mist of the spirit world.

You have such a rich family heritage.

My maternal grandfather was Shawnee and Welsh. My maternal grandmother was Cherokee and Irish. My paternal grandparents were from the Netherlands and Germany. My grandfather had Gypsy in his family.

What types of things do you see in the future?

What I see is like a road map. People have choices in life. I give them insight into their choices. What they choose to do is entirely up to them. Most of my clients are women. I think women see readings more as something that's fun to do and accept it as entertainment. If something I tell them comes true, they'll come back. I don't think men want to believe. They aren't as mystical as women.

Your vision quests have been integral to your life.
What are vision quests?

Vision quests help people decide what they'll do for the rest of their life. When I was 17 I went into the Cumberland Mountains on my first vision quest. I prayed for an animal guiding spirit, a totem, to come to me. Since I'm quite literal, I sat on a mountain, freezing my butt off for a day and a half. When I was half asleep I looked up and was nose to nose with a turtle.

I took it home to my aunt who explained that the Shawnee people had 13 clans, including the turtle clan. They consider the turtle a spiritual creature and believe that someone chosen by the turtle could speak to the spirits. From the turtle I learned I had to come out of my shell and interact with the world.

I began to study cougars after encountering one on my second vision quest. The female raises her children by herself and teaches them to be strong and brave, how to survive. That's what I had to do for my children. Cougars also have a very playful nature with their cubs. I learned from the cougar to have fun and not take everything so seriously.

My third vision quest led me to the spider. To be more precise, a spider web covered my head and a dead spider was between my eyes. From then on I was called Star Spider Woman. The spider signifies creation and the weaving of the above world of the spirits to the below world of humans and animals. Following the death of my second husband, I was very depressed and went on my fourth quest. A mockingbird kept following me around, making me crazy. When I left, a mockingbird wing feather was on my car. The mockingbird taught me that I had to come out and still live.

How did Tarot cards lead to your becoming an author?

I created a Native American Tarot deck that became very popular. A publisher asked me to expand the idea of the Tarot cards into a book about Native American history. It became *Star Spider Speaks: The Teachings of the Native American Tarot.*

What do you like best about yourself?

I'm young at heart. I don't let my age stop me from doing the things I like. I still ride horses and practice swordplay.

Mimi Ha

You've described your childhood in Vietnam as a life of fear.
I was born during the Vietnam War. My father was in the military for 20 years. I was born and raised on an Air Force base. I lived in fear wondering if we would make it through each day.

You and your sister escaped two days before the Communists took over. You weren't even able to tell your mother you were leaving. That must have been heartbreaking.
My older sister was working for the American embassy. She was told she could leave Vietnam with her husband and child, but that her siblings wouldn't be able to go with her. She registered me as her daughter. My father encouraged us to escape but told me not to tell my mother. She probably would not have let us go. I was 13 years old and wanted to go to a better life in the United States, and I hoped we would all one day be together again. It was terribly sad not to be able to tell my mother goodbye. When we left I was afraid I would never see either of my parents again.

For 15 years you had no communication with your parents and they had to report you and your sister missing.
Letters were censored and I didn't want to jeopardize my parents. Once the Communists were in control, my parents had to state that my sister and I were missing. Their lives would have been in danger if they had revealed our escape.

Your fear took on a different character once you arrived in this country. How easily did you adapt to American life?
We joined thousands of people in a refugee camp in Guam and later in one in Pennsylvania. I was scared and wanted to go home but that was impossible. Every time I heard a helicopter it reminded me of the war and bombing at home. We had been taught to drop everything and run into the sandbag-filled cellar when we saw or heard a helicopter.

Months later we were sponsored by a Presbyterian Church in Dayton, Ohio. I started a new life thanks to a wonderful woman who became my foster mother. The first few days in school were a strange experience. I hadn't seen many foreign people when I was growing up in Vietnam. It's kind of funny now, but at the time I thought everybody looked alike. The kids were very nice to me but communicating with them was hard because I spoke and understood only a little English. I hid in my room when guests visited. Soon I realized that everyone was trying to help me with a smooth transition and wouldn't harm me. I was young and adapted relatively quickly. During the winter of 1975 I saw the first snow of my life. I ate it and wanted to stay outside all day. I soon loved many things American, such as food and movies and clothes. The only American clothes I had seen before coming here were in the Sears catalog.

How did you become reunited with your family?
My sister and I sponsored my parents and seven siblings to come to the United States.

Have you been back to Vietnam?
I went back after having been away for 30 years. My mother had warned me that I wouldn't recognize many things about the area in which I grew up. Things have changed so much. War is always destructive, but there has been a great deal of investment in Vietnam. It's a better country now and the Vietnamese have much better lives than they did before.

What do you like best about yourself?
That I have been able to hold it together and have a successful life here after my ordeal in Vietnam. I'm a survivor. I try to be positive. I'm kindhearted and like to go out of my way to help others. I appreciate things in life. I'm a simple girl.

And least?
I sometimes have a hot temper like my mother.

What would people be surprised to know about you?
Once you get to know me I can't stop talking, but I'm very shy about public speaking. And they might be surprised to know that I was a model.

Other than the people in your life, what couldn't you live without?
Hot tea and a quiet time for myself.

If you could be anywhere in the world right now, where would you be and what would you be doing?
I'd be sipping tea on a beach in Hawaii.

Karen Ryan Harris

You're a cat's best friend. Seriously, how did you become involved with Shamrock Pet Foundation?

Our cats were all spayed or neutered. I started fostering pregnant cats for the Animal Care Society so my daughter could see the process and to introduce her to volunteer work. When Shamrock was formed in 1992, they contacted me. I have fostered over a thousand cats and kittens. Litters are my niche. I'm now Chairperson of the Cat Committee.

You have some very special cats in your own home.

Because of personality or health problems, they're unadoptable. But I love them.

Shamrock, and you, take a very definite stand on a couple of cat issues.

Our adoption contract states that the cats will not be allowed outside. Many people don't realize it, but there is a leash law for cats unless they're in your own yard. They can get hit by cars, poisoned, attacked by dogs, and can acquire leukemia or FIV, which are fatal. At the very least they'll get fleas or ear mites. Why would anyone take the risk?

We don't have a lot of sympathy for someone who has an animal they don't want anymore. We try to take animals that are injured or starving or have newborn babies, and put them up for adoption.

Cats can be very loving. Why do people not see that?

Many people like dogs because dogs are predictable and submissive. Even a very affectionate cat is more independent than a dog. You can never tell a cat what to do. Cats usually call the shots. Also, cats are just like human babies. If they don't receive a lot of touching and interaction when they're tiny, they will have personality issues. They need to be handled, even from birth, and even if only for a minute or two at a time. If they have no human interaction by the time they're eight weeks old, they'll probably be feral.

You have had so many success stories with cats. Is there one that particularly stands out?

One of the saddest cases that turned out well involved a nursing mother cat who had been shot in the leg and had her foot blown apart. A vet was able to put her foot back together and she healed well. She was an adorable, sweet cat.

What has been the biggest challenge of your life?

My husband left when my daughter was two months old. It was a huge hurdle, physically, emotionally and mentally. I raised her by myself. My greatest heartbreak turned out to be my greatest joy.

What's the most important thing you've learned about yourself?

I've learned what's worth getting upset about, how to maintain my composure and not fly off the handle, and to think before I act. It takes something really big to get to me.

Other than the people in your life, what couldn't you live without?

Cats and dogs. In addition to my cats, I also have two rescue dogs. I will always have rescue animals. Once you learn how to rescue and adopt, how can you not do it? The need will always be there. It seems to get worse every year despite our efforts to encourage and even pay for spay/neuter.

What traits do you most like in a person?

Honesty and integrity. They go hand in hand. And I admire intelligence. I look up to people who are more knowledgeable than I am.

And least?

Phoniness, lying, cheating, and abusing animals or children.

How do you measure success?

By the impact you have on your family, your work, and the community. You want to leave the world a better place than it was. I know that's a cliché, but it's what I believe.

What would people be surprised to know about you?

I don't have any secrets. I don't try to be anything other than what I am. I'm honest about myself.

How do you feel about aging?

I always use the old Irish proverb: "Do not begrudge growing older. Many are denied the privilege." I don't plan on any cosmetic surgery. I earned these wrinkles and arthritic hands.

What haven't you done that you would like to do?

Nothing. I have no bucket list. I have been everywhere I want to go and have done everything I want to do. I am perfectly happy where I am in my life.

Is there anything that intimidates you?

Being in a book.

Virginia Gray Henry

You have taught world religions around the globe, and you are a publisher of books devoted to world spirituality. Do you believe you were put on earth to help other people discover their spirituality?

Each of us has been given a combination of qualities which come from God who is the Source of all. Each thing in nature is made up of different proportions of Divine characteristics. A tree, for example, manifests verticality, rigor, protectiveness and majesty. A daisy displays qualities of delicacy and childlike simplicity. A deer may be referred to if we wished to explain to another, "What is Grace?" We can say "busy as a bee" or "faithful as a dog" because each animal has fixed qualities. Then, we notice how each of us is different and has varied gifts to give. We cannot take ownership of our character but we can observe what our combination of energies and efforts seems naturally to be aimed at. I am responsible for what is passing through me—using my abilities which I did not give myself. I can see that I have unusual energy, a sense of oneness with people and nature, a great love of spiritual matters, and have been made by God to be an educator and publisher. I am interested in working on my own spiritual nature and the work I do hopefully invites others along what I consider to be the most important path.

Encouraging and supporting the interfaith dialogue must, at times, seem overwhelming. Does the cacophony of voices ever seem to drown out any possible dialogue?

There are two types of people. Literalists take their own scripture to be absolute and may not accept that other faith traditions are loved by God. I have many family members of this persuasion and this is perfectly fine. These dear ones are fulfilling the very qualities of focus with which they have been endowed. Then there are others who feel that God would not have created many faiths if He had not wanted mankind to approach Him in different ways. There are those who are attracted by their nature to metaphor – as in the parables and to mysticism, as with the monastic communities of all faiths.

You were instrumental in arranging the Dalai Lama's visit to Louisville. You say his life has had a dramatic impact on the world because he embodies the qualities of mercy and compassion. Is the world becoming less merciful and compassionate?

The Dalai Lama is a "bodhisattva," which means that he is devoting every living moment of his life to serving all beings in this world, hoping to lessen their suffering. In that sense, he is an example to us all as the world becomes a less merciful place, which it must do, due to the nature of time itself. In the Christian world, we speak of four ages—The Golden, Silver, Bronze, and Lead. In the Eastern world these four ages are called Yugas. The world today is in the last of the four ages—that of Lead, or the kali-yuga. When God manifested the world and said, "Be," and it was, the early people were closer to God and the Spirit. But the life of the world is like a snowball rolling down a hill. As it focuses on and gathers material weight, it goes faster. All one need do is look around at the devotion to the material world today and it is clear why there is so much evil. Evil is merely distance from God. We do not face the end of time but we do live in the end of an age. But in the end of anything is the seed of the new beginning.

There's no shortage of memorable childbirth tales, but yours is exceptionally intriguing.

Crossing North Africa in 1968 in search of spiritual masters, pregnant, camping out in the desert, cooking on a camp burner Nescafe and Knorr soups, we reached Libya. Near the Egyptian border we stopped so my daughter could be born. At dawn, several Bedouin ladies drinking mint tea, as call to prayer rang out from a minaret, stood by as I sat on the edge of a table and caught my baby as she emerged! A few hours later, I went for a picnic in the mountains where Libyan ladies and I sat nursing our young on a Persian carpet under fig trees. The people of the Middle East have had the greatest influence on me because they truly copy a prophetic norm in their generosity—always putting the other first. I had never seen anything like that in my life.

Louisa Weeks Henson

In the 1970s and 1980s, you were regarded as Louisville's Queen of Rock and Roll. That's exciting!

I co-owned and co-managed top-rated radio station WLRS for 16 years with my brother Ed. He and I were part of the management team of a broadcasting company that owned and operated seven radio stations. Those were exhilarating times. One of my goals is to write the memoirs of WLRS.

You're credited for keeping MTV out of the Louisville market for quite some time. That must have been an interesting power play.

Our company introduced music videos to Louisville. We knew MTV was coming into Louisville, but we wanted to concentrate on local programming. We created cable channel WLRS –TV 10. We had one staff person who shot film footage of Louisville and would simulcast it with the radio station broadcasting behind that.

And you were a record producer?

It was a real community event. We produced eight albums featuring Louisville musicians. Local artists designed the album covers, and I wrote the insert.

Why are you sad about the current state of local radio and television?

Both radio and television are owned by conglomerates, and that's extremely sad. The radio business is now satellite feeds and computer programming. The disc jockeys record most of their comments. There's little live local programming anymore. Local programming should be creative and avant-garde. It should be appropriate to and reflective of the community, but that isn't the case in Louisville, at all.

Your company was also famous for spectacularly lighting a bridge and producing a fireworks display that spawned Thunder Over Louisville.

We thought it would be different to light the Big Four Bridge for the holidays. LG&E donated the cable, and the National Guard used their helicopters to put the 900-pound coils of cable on the top of the bridge. The project became Bridge the Gap which led to a radiothon for the toy campaign. The radiothon continued for more than ten years and raised hundreds of thousands of dollars.

We also produced the first fireworks display on the Ohio River with Zambelli Internationale which led, years later, to Thunder Over Louisville.

Bridge the Gap has become an important Louisville not-for-profit.

It's a family-owned charity that's very grass roots-oriented. Although it started out as a toy and food campaign, it has evolved into assisting a variety of organizations and individuals. We have funded a community center library, built handicap ramps, assisted refugee families, and helped flood victims and cancer patients. We don't really confine our involvement to one type of project.

You've been an integral part of the growth and evolution of Louisville. Are you pleased with the city now?

Yes and no. I am thrilled and proud of the development of the Big Four Bridge into a pedestrian walkway. That has been a longtime personal dream. I regret that some of the local festivals, in particular the Bluegrass Festival, have not continued. It had age, heritage, and national acclaim. I think it's possible to compete and grow but still keep local flavor. Whether or not we have done that is another question.

What traits do you most like in a person?

Honesty, a sense of humor, and loyalty.

And least?

Mean streaks.

What might people be surprised to know about you?

When I was 23, I had an acoustic neuroma brain tumor. It left me deaf in my right ear.

What do you think helped define who you are?

My father was a perfectionist and I inherited some of that. My inclination for perfectionism can drive me crazy. My mother was a very strong person and also believed in women's rights. She was so proud of the accomplishments of my sister Susan and myself. I still feel I have to meet my parents' expectations. But both my father and mother helped in the most positive ways to determine who I am.

Any regrets?

That I didn't have children of my own. But ten years ago my husband and I sponsored a family from Kosovo. The family's two girls, my six nieces and nephews and my four step children are all in the center of my heart.

Do you think you have "found" yourself?

I have contentment. But I'm never totally content. There's juxtaposition for you.

How do you feel about aging?

It's going to be interesting. I'm not afraid of it. My mother had a plague that said old age isn't for sissies, and I agree. I want to grow old naturally. No nips and tucks for me. I don't want staples in my head.

Ingrid Hernández

As owner of your own graphic design firm, is it difficult to balance your creative side with paying attention to the bottom line?
I struggle with it. I hope to become more involved on the creative side. I'm always concentrating on how to break through the clutter. We have to continually evolve and change the ways we communicate with people. We can't capture an audience with only one type of communication. And we have to figure out creative ways to reach different audiences.

You are certified as a woman-and-minority-owned business. Have you found that being a Latina has made it easier or has it made it more difficult to succeed in your business? Or has it not mattered?
It really hasn't mattered. But the fact that I'm bilingual has been a huge benefit for my business.

I work hard and believe that always pays off regardless of color or gender. But, a client once questioned me, in front of 50 people, whether I really owned the business. He was very disrespectful and harsh. And it was made worse because he was a person of color.

One of the services your company offers is branding. Would you ever help brand a company or product you didn't believe in?
I wouldn't work with something that goes against my values. For example, I'm very against smoking so I wouldn't be able to have a tobacco client.

What has been the most defining moment in your life?
I had just lost my mom to cancer, lost my job, and lost the dream of having a baby. All of that led to starting my own business. It's the best thing I've ever done.

So, starting your business has been your most significant accomplishment?
That and helping raise three stepchildren. I know I made a positive difference in their lives.

Other than the people in your life, what couldn't you live without?
Shoes. I'm only five feet tall, so I like that they make me feel tall. One of my dreams is to do work for a shoe company.

Is there anything that intimidates you?
Dealing with difficult people when they're deliberately trying not to be nice. I don't know where they're coming from. I'm a giving person and hate confrontation. However, I will say things that need to be said, but never in a

mean way, always in a pleasant way. When I have to deal with really tough situations I always consult with experts and get their backup. I like to seek the right advice and support.

What's the most important thing you've learned about yourself?
That I can do it.

In three or four words, how would you describe yourself?
Confident, caring, and creative.

Any regrets?
None. Everything is a learning experience, good or bad.

What would people be surprised to know about you?
I'm pretty daring. In New Zealand I jumped off a cliff using a parachute.

What haven't you done that you would like to do?
One of my short-term goals is to learn to cook. Long-term, I want to travel to Australia and to parts of Asia where I haven't been.

How do you feel about aging?
I'm not afraid of it. Our family has good genes. My father is in his 80s and has no wrinkles. How lucky is that?

You describe yourself as a perfectionist. Is that a good or bad thing?
It's both good and bad. It's good in the sense that you keep working on something until you are 200 percent satisfied with it. Clients see the difference when you do this and they appreciate it. It's bad if you don't know when to stop working on something.

What do you like to do in your free time?
Weight training, yoga, salsa dancing, art shows, traveling for pleasure or to visit my family in Puerto Rico, spending time with friends at a local gourmet restaurant or community events, sponsoring events or helping with fundraising efforts for charities dear to my hear, and helping my family or friends any way I can.

Finish the sentence, "I wish women would….
make education a priority so they can accomplish their dreams, be strong and independent, and become an inspiration to other women."

Peggy Heuser

Although you are now extremely successful and happy, your early life was extremely difficult.

I came from a very dysfunctional family. My mother thrived on turmoil. If there was peace, she wasn't happy. I'm one of six children; two of us are good and four are bad. Some of them simply are awful people. My siblings have a variety of problems, including dependency issues of drugs and alcohol. I was able to extricate myself from all that by getting out of the house when I was growing up. I didn't get caught up in what was happening at home because I was gone swimming all the time or being very involved in a leadership capacity at school.

Now you're a partner in the Heuser Clinic, which provides programs using nutrition and exercise. What are your roles in the clinic?

I'm a registered nurse. I do health risk assessments on our patients. Also, as Chief Operating Officer, I run the day-to-day operations. And I oversee the marketing and recruitment, and do the fundraising for the Louisville Youth Training Center, our not-for-profit.

How did you become so involved in nutrition and exercise?

My husband Lou and I are former athletes and have always had an interest in staying well and fit. We've taken seven family vacations on bicycles. In order to live the lifestyle we love, we have to be fit. I never wanted to get out of shape. I exercised up to the day I delivered both of my children and was back exercising within two weeks after they were born.

I worked as a nurse in the operating room with my husband, who was chief of surgery at Norton Hospital. We saw patients on a daily basis who were unhealthy secondary to their surgical problems. They were almost all overweight and often were prediabetic and had serious heart issues. At the same time, we were noticing how many of our children's friends were overweight. We decided to open the clinic because of the magnitude of the problem.

Why are young people such a focus of your programs?

It's so much easier to prevent a child from becoming obese than dealing with the problem once it develops. If children go through puberty overweight, they have a 90 percent chance of being overweight for life. However, if they're already obese as children, there's still a much greater chance of turning it around than waiting until they're adults. We know that if children are exposed to nutrition and exercise, it can be lifelong learning with real-world experience.

You're a guru of healthy eating and cooking and are very conscious of what's in every bite you take. You also frequently host parties, both small and large. Do you think guests eat before they come just in case the menu is full of healthy ingredients but short on taste?

No! We serve delicious meals full of amazing flavor. People look forward to our parties because they know they'll get a meal that tastes great and that won't kill them. There's really no reason for anyone to feel deprived when they eat a healthy diet. It's just a matter of changing recipes to use healthy ingredients.

Be honest. Don't you sometimes crave a Big Mac or some junk food?

I will be honest. Sometimes we go to a party where the food is so bad we can't choke it down. Lou and I will wink at each other knowing what's coming. We leave the party, head for White Castle, and eat the bad food we like, not the bad food we don't like.

In a few words, how would you describe yourself?

Disciplined, optimistic, dependable, and very hard-working. I'm devoted to whatever I'm doing.

What do you like best about yourself?

I enjoy life and try to have fun almost every day. It could be work or it could be fundraising. I hope what drives me is good for others.

And least?

I wish I could learn to be less impulsive with my emotions.

Have you "found" yourself?

I'm getting there. I know who I am. I'm learning to like myself more. I never thought much about it before. But you know, once your children are grown and move away, you look at your own life, what you've accomplished and what you want to do.

What's the best decision you have ever made?

Hands down, marrying my husband. He's truly my partner and best friend. Because we work together, I spend every day with him. I dread what either one of us will do without the other.

Holly Holland

You're an accomplished journalist and author. To what do you contribute your success?

I believe my gift is as a storyteller, finding a representative story that conveys information to people. I'm good at being a fly on the wall and at asking good questions that allow people to talk about something they care about.

How did yoga become such an important part of your life?

After a career in journalism and publishing, I developed terrible physical issues—an adrenal insufficiency, fibromyalgia, and pneumonia. My husband suggested I try yoga. I scoffed at the idea because I thought it was sedentary and not fast-paced enough for me. But yoga was intriguing to me because I was interested in how people relax. Because of yoga and, subsequently, Pilates, I feel better than at any time in my life. They have had such a transformative effect on me. The knowledge of the mind/body connection is profound. When you have the knowledge it changes everything about the way you move, sleep, and interact with people.

Have people told you that you exude energy and passion?

Sometimes my energy and passion wear me out, and they probably wear out other people, as well. My son complains that everything is a priority with me. I'm impatient. I want to jump in and take charge, often sooner than I should. I'm a good creator and a good rallier. When I believe in something, I'm not shy about sharing it. I'm really good at touching one life and letting those ripples go in the water. Also, I'm a really good friend. I care very deeply about my relationships and I'm enriched by my friends.

What motivates you?

I came of age at the cusp of the women's movement. I saw fences broken down by people before me, so I felt a duty to do my part and take charge of things. I believe I was put here to do good, and it's something I have to rise to every day.

You've said that other than your family, the work you do with the Lost Boys of Sudan is what makes you most proud.

A service committee at Thomas Jefferson Unitarian Church made a presentation about the Lost Boys. Church groups were asked to sponsor a group of refugees for three months. I was so moved by the story of these children raising themselves. That spoke to me as a mother of two boys. I said I would lead the effort for the church. We were going to sponsor four boys. That group grew to dozens. They had never lived in the modern world, but when they came here they were completely dedicated to living here and to getting an

education. I became Mom to them. We started offering scholarships through the Community Foundation. More than half of the boys have been admitted to college or have received degrees. Many worked full time while going to school, and some sent relatives in Sudan to school.

You don't mince words when it comes to your views about education.

I love to write about education. When you give someone an education, you can never take it away from them. Schools are our prime civic institution. I'm always amazed that many people think they're education experts, that they know how to run the schools. They wouldn't think they could run a hospital just because they've been a patient in one. Traditionally, we haven't done a good job of explaining what happens in schools and how it affects our kids and the community.

Are you content with your life?

I feel very comfortable at this stage in my life, but I'm not a complacent person. I love the learning curve and think that's what keeps us young. I know there's always a new phase and a new challenge. Aging bothers me only in that I can notice the body doesn't respond quite as well. I'm hoping I can learn enough about it that I can age gracefully. I don't care about getting wrinkles, but I care about maintaining my energy indefinitely because I have a lot to do.
.

What's next for you?

I'd like to work overseas. My husband and I have talked about going to an area that hasn't been served well. We want to go beyond this environment. Maybe I'll do something with writing and yoga and teaching. Who knows how that will play out, but people are hungry for attention. I think you can change the world when you respond to that. Looking at the world, everything seems overwhelming. You have to start with one person. It's very powerful when you can touch someone else's life.

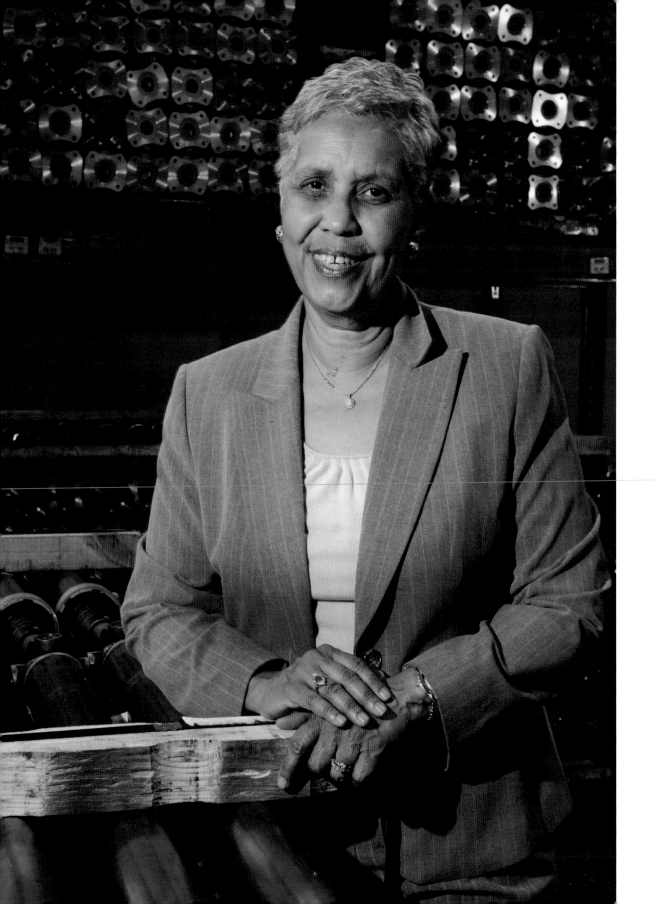

Alice Houston

You and your husband Wade were partners in the second largest minority business in the United States. Now you're President and CEO of Houston-Johnson, a trucking and logistics company. Those are very impressive accomplishments.

The automotive industry was one of the first to support and recognize that it makes good business sense to have a diverse supplier base. We were fortunate enough to be part of that initial thrust, and fortunate that we were in the right place at the right time, with the right sets of skills and entrepreneurial drive. But we also had to be willing to take the risk.

I had great role models, and education was stressed in my family. I had prepared myself. But today there are young people, especially talented young women and minorities, who have prepared themselves, but the opportunities aren't there. What my generation faced in the '60s was nothing like the slavery and lynchings that people before me suffered. Having been so close to people who went through those things, I felt tremendous responsibility and I was very determined to be a success and to help others along their way. You can't just pack your bag and go home. Even now we don't have the right to close our doors and hoard our success.

What has it been like to be one of the only women in a male dominated field?

Maybe it's my own internal perception that I have to have a greater sense of accountability and responsibility. It's almost as if I have to prove myself, as a woman and as a minority, to show that I can compete. Perhaps I bring the pressure on myself, but I do feel the added pressure.

My training in counseling and professional development helped me navigate the waters and deal with the difficulties I encountered because of being a woman and a minority. Also, I grew up in an athletic environment. My father was the winningest high school coach in Kentucky, and Wade was assistant basketball coach at U of L and head coach at the University of Tennessee. I learned resilience and the agonizing feeling of defeat. But I also learned that tomorrow is another day and it brings the opportunity for another game.

Allan, your son, was a major NBA star, and your husband was one of the most well known coaches in basketball. Did you ever get used to their fame even though you played a critical role in their success?

I am still Allan's mother and Wade's wife. And that's okay. I'm proud to be both.

Other than the people in your life, what couldn't you live without?

My faith. It allows me to take risks knowing there is nothing I can fail at. It puts life and material things in perspective. I don't know how people live without faith.

You have faced some major challenges. Which one was most difficult?

Watching and caring for aging parents. Seeing the people who had been so instrumental in my life, and working that into the dynamics of our family, were both wonderful and difficult experiences. We could have someone 101 years old and another person who was a week old in our house.

What do you like best about yourself?

My ability to not become frustrated when I manage and embrace different things at home, in business and with my family.

Looking back over your experiences, what's the most important thing you've learned about yourself?

That I can do things I never thought I could do, or even wanted to do. And that I am a lifetime learner.

What would people be surprised to know about you?

That while I'm an early riser, my clock winds down and I become another person about 9:00 at night. Just get out of my way. All of my outgoing friendliness disappears.

How do you feel about aging?

I wouldn't want to go back to my 20s. Bill Cosby's wife Camille never dyed her hair. When I was in my early 30s, my decision not to color my hair was because of her and how she looked. The physical part of aging doesn't bother me. What I fear is losing my mental acumen.

What haven't you done that you want to do?

My bucket list includes going to Africa and China.

How do you measure success?

By how people will think about me after I'm gone, and what impact I will have made on their lives. I think about that in terms of my mother and father. Not a month goes by that someone doesn't tell a story of how my parents impacted other peoples' lives.

Heidi Hulon, D.V.M.

What's most rewarding about being a veterinarian?

Helping animals, because they can't tell you where it hurts. I'm always touched and amazed by the connection we have with animals. There's so much that's revealed by their eyes---whether they're happy, scared or in pain. Also, there's nothing like helping maintain the bond between an animal and its owner.

You've owned an animal clinic, have worked in academia and have been a consultant for animal nutrition and health. But you say there's something else that's especially important to you.

One of the most rewarding things I've done is to work with animals at the Kentucky Humane Society. They're the animals who desperately need to be loved but aren't. It's so hard to see all of them come in through no fault of their own. It's completely a people problem because people fail to understand or to take responsibility for caring for another living creature.

There also have been animals in your care for whom being extremely pampered was a way of life.

While I was in vet school I took care of Sunshine, a baby camel, who had broken her leg. She belonged to a family that had a lot of exotic animals. The television the family sent for her stall was on all day. She also drank special sun tea. Sunshine was adorable but she was quite the brat and diva.

You persevered through such a frightening, traumatic time.

I went through some terrible experiences at the hands of my ex-husband who was physically and abusive to me and to the children. I certainly can understand how that could make someone want to run and hide and live in fear, but that wasn't and isn't me. I decided not to miss out on my life and took control of it for the first time. I'm the happiest I've ever been. It was probably one of the best things that happened to me because I grew as a person. I am now comfortable with who I am and realize what is important in life. My advice for people is not to settle for anything less than what they deserve and to do what makes them happy.

What's the best decision you ever made?

I knew from the age of five that I wanted to be a vet. A big, orange horse named Derby and his pony friend lived on the horse farm that backed up to our property. They were always waiting for me when I got home from kindergarten and first grade. That began a lifelong fascination with and love of animals. So, the best decision I ever made was to go to vet school. Not everyone encouraged that. My mother wasn't at all supportive. Because she didn't understand what I

wanted to do, that meant it was wrong. I wouldn't be able to live with myself if I were the kind of person she wanted me to be. She and I are estranged. It's sad, but it was her choice. I want my kids to do what they love and what they're good at and what makes them proud. I try to show them it isn't always easy and that you have to make sacrifices. Life is too short not to follow your heart.

What do you like best about yourself?

I think I'm funny. And I'm a very caring person. I want to help other people because so many people helped me. They were my angels who kept me up instead of letting me down.

And least?

I'm too nice, so I get walked on. I'm a pleaser and I overextend myself because I don't want to hurt anyone's feelings.

What traits do you dislike in other people?

Pretentiousness and arrogance. And I don't like controlling or hypercritical people.

Is there something people would be surprised to learn about you?

I don't eat green food. I almost choked on a Brussels sprout when I was young.

What haven't you done that you would like to do?

I'd love to go to Europe. Maybe someday I'll open up my own animal behavior clinic. Mostly I just want to watch my kids grow up. And I'd like to fall in love and share a life with someone.

What would you do if you weren't a veterinarian?

I'd be a tennis player or a dancer.

Jeanne James

The Godfather hit close to home for you!

As an FBI agent, I worked bank robberies, motorcycle gangs, white collar crime—you name it, I did it. But one job was out of the ordinary even for me. For two years I worked undercover as a waitress in a Kansas City restaurant that was a front for the Mafia. I met almost every Mafia leader in the United States because they had many of their meetings in the restaurant.

Did you ever worry you might end up in a river?

One time I was a little worried when I thought I had blown my cover. One guy kept telling me what they do to snitches. Thankfully, it turned out I hadn't been discovered after all.

But the "bosses" had a big plan in mind for you.

The godfather in that area picked me out a husband. That's when I told the Bureau I'd do most anything for them, but I wasn't willing to marry into the Mob. We came up with a story that my fiancée had accepted a job somewhere else and I had to go with him. Out of town I went.

Your career with the FBI was full of excitement. You've said once you got a taste of law enforcement, you never looked back.

I got college credit for interning with a police department. I loved it from the first minute. I went on to attend the Tallahassee Police Academy. I had never fired a gun before. I thought if I just watched and learned, no one would be the wiser. I had a misfire on the first round. I ran backward about 90 miles an hour. I soon learned to shoot after my teacher, an FBI agent, took me under his wing. Later, after working as a police officer, I applied to the FBI and was accepted, being one of the first women hired not as a token. There were 10 women in the class. Six didn't make it through. It was rough going.

After the near miss of becoming a Mafia wife, what did you do in the FBI?

I became part of the white collar crime squad in L.A. I also did some counterintelligence. I was on the team that convicted R.W. Miller, the first FBI agent convicted of espionage. After that I transferred to be the head of the FBI's fugitive task force in Louisville. It was probably fairly dangerous but fun at the same time. When you're in the middle of something it doesn't seem as dangerous as it does when you look back on the experience.

You were also a federal air marshal, not the cushiest of jobs.

I was on the planes to avert a terrorist incident. Fortunately that never happened. The job did have its humorous aspects. On a flight from Brazil to Haiti all the passengers were carrying live chickens. The closest I ever came to taking action on a plane was when a man drank too much and became disruptive. The other air marshal and I didn't want to reveal our identities because we were there for possible terrorists. Fortunately the flight attendant got him to sit down.

What's the story behind you, Betty White and Watergate figure G. Gordon Liddy?

I was on the game show *Password*. Betty and G. Gordon were my celebrity partners. It was his first public appearance after he got out of prison. It made the national news—"FBI agent paired with G. Gordon Liddy on Game Show." I can't say enough about Betty; she was so sweet and lovely. G. Gordon was intimidatingly intelligent and also very nice. I didn't win the match but I didn't go home empty-handed. I received consolation prizes of $500, a washer and dryer, a vacuum cleaner, and a case of Lee Press-on Nails.

Is there something you haven't done that you'd like to do?

I'm toying with writing a book. It would be fiction. My main character would be the illegitimate daughter of J. Edgar Hoover. I'd tie in some of the crazy things I've seen over the years.

What's the best decision you ever made?

Marrying my husband seems the nice thing to say, but being a police officer was the best decision. Those years were the best of my life. It was such fun to follow my dream although I almost starved to death.

What traits do you most like in a person?

Honesty, authenticity, intelligence, and kindness.

What would you like to change about yourself?

I'd like to be less scattered. I have too many interests. Sometimes I spread myself too thinly.

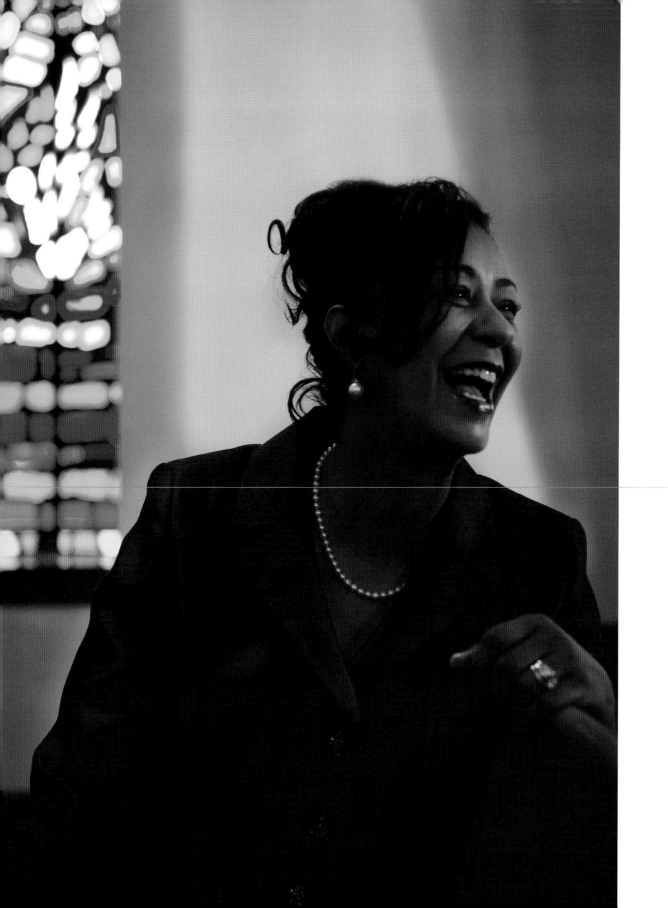

JoAnn James

You bring a very personal perspective to your job as a social worker with the Jefferson County Public School system.

I dropped out of school because of our financial situation and my teen pregnancy. It was my responsibility, not anyone else's, including the government's, to take care of my child. The option of giving up a baby had never been discussed in my family. And I had always said I wanted to live, not just quote the Scriptures. I didn't want to be a hypocrite. I went on to get my GED and then a bachelor's and master's degree in social work.

Whenever teenagers come to me about their pregnancies, I believe God has placed me there to discuss, not judge. They already come with their answer.

Being a social worker must be as rewarding as it is heartbreaking and frustrating.

Yes, because there are so many components to it. I visit families at home and encourage collaboration between the school, parents, and community. My work focuses on the huge problem of truancy. It's so complicated because of issues within families, such as divorce and illness, and in too many cases, the absence of valuing an education. Sometimes there's a stigma associated with social workers and some parents may feel that I'm coming to get their children. But most parents are very understanding and cooperative because they know I'm there to empower them. They don't feel like it's them against us. It can be terribly sad when the children don't even have food and the house is in awful condition. I have to take a holistic approach and coordinate with agencies to provide childcare, medical care, and other services.

Is it difficult to separate your feelings from your work?

The separation comes through prayer and the understanding of my role. I have the knowledge and information to help people. And I know that I left the family better than I found them.

You're also a pastor's wife. That can't be easy.

A pastor's wife lives in a fishbowl. I love it. It fits in perfectly with my social work. My partnership with my husband has kept me in touch with what's going on with families. My role with him is to help our ministry stay on the forefront of the social needs as well as the spiritual needs of a family. And I love the ministry that has changed so much over the last 25 years. It's now not only Sunday and Wednesday, but it's also about youth ministry, women's and men's Bible studies, even line dancing and exercise class.

What drives you?

I want to live my purpose for God. I don't want to disappoint Him.

How would you describe yourself?

Fun, loving, caring, and inspirational. I like to hang out with girlfriends, eat, share stories, and celebrate each other. I'm very selective about my energy circle.

You've been married for 25 years. What's the key to a good marriage?

Prayer, lots of prayer. And flexibility.

What's the best decision you ever made?

I can't choose just one. There are three—going back to school, getting married, and having my children.

What, other than the people in your life, couldn't you live without?

The Bible and my phone.

If you weren't a social worker, what would you like to do?

Something in the art world, either writing or painting. I hope to have an opportunity to explore that.

Who is the most fascinating woman you know or know about?

Again, it's impossible to make only one choice. It would be the women in my immediate family because of their stories, their ability to survive, and the respect I have for their legacies.

What do you like best about yourself?

My personality and my ability to see the good in all situations. But I think there are people who are evil at their core.

What traits do you most like in a person?

Their inner spirit, not their outer beauty.

And what do you dislike in a person?

The cruel words they can say.

Is there something you would change about yourself if you could?

I need to challenge myself to become more knowledgeable about money and the business world.

What haven't you done that you would like to do?

I want to go to Africa and to the Holy Land.

How do you feel about aging?

I love it. It has some humor, and I'm embracing it.

U. Geetha Joseph,
M.D.

Your own experience gave you a special perspective on your work as an oncologist/hematologist.

I was eight months pregnant and was planning to train in oncology. My husband, also a doctor, was diagnosed with leukemia. We were crushed. I had way too much information to be comfortable. I thought it would have been nice if I had not known as much as I did about his disease. He had a successful bone marrow transplant and completely recovered. When I realized he was going to survive I felt so blessed. I have always thought there must be some reason that he survived and we were able to continue as a family. I'm a doctor during the day but I also try to give back in other ways. I'm very involved with the Leukemia and Lymphoma Society. It's the least I can do for how lucky we were.

Too often science doesn't have the answers and you have to tell patients that there's no cure for them.

That's the art of medicine. No one can teach you how to do it. Some will ask if they're going to die or how much time they have to live. Others don't ask the question. I always let them know whether or not their illness is curable and I offer statistics. There's a pit in my stomach every time I have to give such devastating news, watching someone's whole life shatter.

Do you ever cry with your patients?

I try not to cry because it takes away their hope. But I cry at the end of their life. Some people have told me the most incredible things at the end. They've smiled and thanked me and told me they'll see me in the next world. It is such a privilege throughout the process to be able to help them make their journey easier.

Extraordinary medical advances have enabled many of your patients to have their disease completely eradicated, and for you to share with them a look at their future.

Oh, yes! That's what keeps us going. There has been much progress in many areas. We're now able to target a specific area without causing harm to normal tissues. It's like a guided missile that kills only the tumor.

You're no stranger to what must seem like miracles.
Do you believe in God?

Yes. There has to be something better after this life on earth. It's very hard for me to believe this is the end.

How do men and women differ in the way they cope with serious illness?

In general, I think women are stronger in that they are better able to deal with death and dying. Women verbalize their feelings. Men don't want to talk about bad things; they'd rather try to ignore them although the feelings are still there. Usually when men come into the office their wives are with them. But women frequently come with their sisters and friends because it's easier for them to talk to other women.

How do you deal with the stress of your work?

I find it very relaxing to sing in my church choir. And I started oil painting about a year and a half ago. All my stresses disappear in the painting class.

What haven't you done that you'd like to do?

Spend the winters volunteering with clinical trials in India. There are so many patients there but the doctors are overworked. And there are so many resources that haven't been tapped into.

Do you have any regrets?

That I didn't have more children. Also, because my work is very demanding, I gave up a lot of time with my daughter. I hope I did a good job juggling being a doctor with being a mother, but sometimes I think I did a better job in medicine.

Have you "found" yourself?

If I found myself, I don't know what I'd do for the rest of my life.

What would people be surprised to know about you?

I'm a dancing queen. My cell phone ring tone is set to *Dancing Queen* by Abba. I went to a Beach Boys concert a few years ago. I was dancing up and down the aisle. The couple next to me watched and smiled at me. The next Monday they were in my office, and said they had loved to see me dancing and enjoying myself, that it showed a very human side to me.

How do you feel about aging?

It's wonderful to age, and if you're lucky, you do it gracefully. Don't fight it. Go with the flow. There are so many worse things than aging.

Terri Kendall

First, you took a circus class. Now you're an aerial artist.
I metamorphosed into my own style, which is kind of raw and edgy. I'm very athletic. My specialty is doing tricks on a rope, up in the air 10 to 25 feet. I also work on the trapeze, and with rings and with an aerial pole.

You're a valet with Ohio Valley Wrestling. For those of us without a clue, what is a valet?
A valet escorts the wrestlers to and from the ring, cheers them on, comforts them, cheats for them, and heckles the other wrestlers. We also distract and flirt with the referee and even hit the other wrestlers. I'm starting to train as a wrestler. I might be past the age range for wrestling, but there are some things I'll be able to do.

But there are also several other sides to you.
Yes, I'm finishing my 18th year as a school psychologist. I feel like I have been very successful at it. Because I have so many irons in the fire, I get overwhelmed. I love to train. I get up and do cardio, lift weights in the afternoon, and do aerials in the evening. But I'm also kind of geeky. I read all the time. I'm very driven. Trying to learn boundaries has been one of my issues since I've been in my 40s. I'm a bit of a rescuer and want everyone to be happy.

You've been diagnosed with a mood disorder and have suffered from bulimia. How have you dealt with those issues?
I have bipolar characteristics without being fully manic. I was bulimic for many years but finally got help for it. I poured myself into therapy and into recovering. It was like the devil because you can't just stay away from food. One never fully recovers from those problems, but I deal with them by sticking to my lifestyle, working out, eating super clean, having no sugar, taking vitamins, and meditating. When I feel dysfunctional thinking coming up, I reach out better and get together with friends. I don't trust myself to be alone when I feel like that.

What has been the biggest challenge in your life?
I can't seem to crack the code with intimate relationships. I feel like guys want to put me in a certain box that I don't want to be in. They sometimes look at me as an object, so I often stay away from them. But I want a relationship and am open to suggestions about how to have one!

And the most defining moment in your life?
I changed inside and began my transformation when I broke up with a guy who was an alcoholic, and I started weight lifting six days a week. I was 29 or 30 years old. I became empowered and was no longer a victim.

How do you measure success?
I'm a bright, positive spirit in this world, and people recognize that. They like that I'm around them because I've done something that has inspired them.

What would people be surprised to know about you?
Even though I seem so strong and independent, I have a kind of neediness that makes me want someone special in my life.

Other than the people in your life, what couldn't you live without?
My athleticism saves me. When I'm totally bumming and feel insecure, it makes me feel good and sets me apart.

What has been the most significant accomplishment of your life?
That I raised two kids and got an education on my own. I've come out of it okay and I feel so blessed that my girls are well-adjusted, healthy, beautiful, intelligent, and creative.

Is there anything that intimidates you?
Relationships. To have someone have power or control over my feelings.

What do you like best about yourself?
My resiliency. No matter what happens, I come out strong. I don't let things get me down, and I don't become jaded or bitter.

Finish the sentence, "I wish women would….
know that they can reach for their dreams no matter what their age."

Looking ahead, what's next for you?
I'd like to get into motivational speaking and focus on physical and mental health. I might like to work with teenage girls, although I also want to inspire all people, particularly women, to understand that they can be physically and mentally healthy and don't have to put up obstacles. I want to help them be themselves.

Nana Lampton

From the perspective of a painter and poet, how do you see the world?
There's so much sadness and misfortune in the world that makes you ache. The job of the artist is to show the brighter, more creative part of us that can someway help people to cure and heal. I write and paint not to get away from the world, but to connect more to it. A lot of emotion is in both my poetry and my paintings. When you're in the right state of mind, there's an open channel between the heart and the brush or the pen.

A poet tries to see past borders, obstacles, and appearances. My poems respond to our local, global, and cosmic situations. My paintings are very much the same.

You've earned a place among some of the most respected executives in the country. You serve on several boards and are chair and CEO of American Life and Accident Insurance Company of Kentucky and of its parent company, Hardscuffle. You've served three terms as director of The Committee of 200, an organization of leading businesswomen from around the world. Is it difficult for an artist to be a leader in the corporate world
Art and business need to come together. My life melds the two. I enjoy living in both worlds and weaving together the corporate and artistic pieces of my life. Some of my most wonderful experiences have been centered around business. The original purpose of the trip doesn't matter. What matters is that you observe.

Why has your involvement in The Committee of 200 been so meaningful to you?
It has had a major influence on me because it helped me understand that I could persevere and if I did persevere that I could learn enough to run a good company.

What's been the major challenge in your life?
Learning to be an independent woman without simple obedience to stronger people. It was difficult for men to take me seriously. I had to prove myself. But times have changed so much for women. There are now thousands of women contending for leadership jobs.

As a member of the board of directors of Constellation Energy Group, which owns and operates nuclear power plants, you must find yourself at the center of considerable controversy.
We work with 800 people who are running nuclear power that generates one-fifth of the power of the country. Wind and solar comprise only 1 percent of energy. We're trying to be extremely knowledgeable and careful about how

nuclear power works. I've been a student of that for 17 years. I hope to be involved in nuclear power after my board membership ends.

And you're a farmer!
I have five farms along the river. Five men and I work together to manage them and keep the cows happy. The farm is the source of much of my painting. Humans need to be connected to the earth.

Is that also why you're on the board of the Bluegrass Conservancy?
Yes. It's the region's only private, nonprofit land trust working to protect the natural diversity, scenic open space, rural heritage, and agricultural vitality of the Bluegrass Region through land conservation for the benefit of the public.

What has been your major disappointment?
The lack of a long-lasting relationship. I don't know if it is a disappointment or part of the labor toward independence. I think it has been worth it. My generation is the first to give any approval to a woman living alone. The idea of not being married still has a social flag on it, but I don't feel it so much because I come and go as I wish.

What are the biggest risks you've ever taken?
Leaving a marriage and, secondly, taking on debt.

Is there anything that intimidates you?
I'm in awe of great knowledge.

What, other than the people in your life, couldn't you live without?
The land, the earth.

What's one of the most important things you've learned?
It's important to spend the little time you have with people who will enrich your life.

Finish the sentence, "I wish…..
that I had discovered sooner that I could have confidence."

How do you feel about aging?
I'm happy about it. If we're lucky, aging goes along with wisdom. There's discovery and seeing things you didn't see before.

Penny Love

You were one of Louisville's first female builders. Do you consider yourself sort of a pioneer?

Well, I'm certainly one of the few that have lasted for 18 years. I have seen a lot of women come and go over the years. It's basically a man's business. I had been involved mostly in interior design for about 15 years although I had feelings about the overall look of homes. I got up one day and thought, "I've always wanted to build, so I'm going to do it." The worst thing that could have happened is that I would have lost money. I figured if I didn't succeed, I'd quit.

When you were entering such a male-dominated field, did you encounter people who didn't support you or hindered your success?

Absolutely. There were peers, suppliers, and subcontractors who questioned my credibility simply because I was a woman. Since they didn't give me a chance in the beginning, once I became successful I decided to use other people. There was one exception. He and I have talked many times about his initial reaction to me. Over the years, we have become good friends and he has a lot of faith in everything I do. I believe part of my success can be attributed to the fact that I work as a team with the people who work for me.

You're not getting out of the building business, but you're going to be expressing your creativity in a completely new way.

I can walk through a house in my mind, even before there's anything on paper. Or I can look at a house plan and envision the finished result. I can do the same things when I look at semiprecious and precious stones. I have always loved the creativity of jewelry, so I'm starting to design and make jewelry. I'm excited about a new adventure.

What has been the most defining moment in your life?

My first husband died at a very young age in a car accident. That changed the dynamics of everything.

What has been the biggest challenge in your life?

Stepping into the home building business when I was single. I wanted it so much. I was eating, sleeping, and drinking my job, and still do to a certain extent. To be successful, you have to love what you're doing, and I did from day one. It will be time to quit when the passion is gone.

Other than the people in your life, what couldn't you live without?

Harley and Mulligan, our Wheaten terriers.

What would people be surprised to know about you?

I'm not very tech-savvy. I struggle with that. The whole world seems to revolve around electronics, but I don't.

How would you describe yourself in a few words?

I'm a people-pleaser. And I'm positive and very happy.

Is there anything you'd like to change about yourself?

I'm troubled that I don't speak up and voice my opinion as much as I should. I have had to learn how to be more forceful while still being tactful. But, there's a limit to my forcefulness. In business, as well as in my relationship with my husband, I've learned that I can't fix something if I don't know what to fix. I have to be able to express what's bothering me, get it on the table, and move on.

How would you finish the sentence, "I wish women would…

always stand up for what they believe regardless of anyone else's opinion."

What traits do you most like in a person?

An even temperament, predictability, and the desire to really be happy.

And least?

Volatility and unpredictability.

How do you feel about aging?

When my birthday rolls around, I'm just tickled to be here. I'm in good health and am happier with each day because I appreciate life in such a different way than when I was younger. I try to be even more compassionate and thoughtful. I reach out to people and let them know I care and think about them.

What haven't you done that you would like to do?

I'd like to become an architect or a chef. If I studied to be an architect, I might be one of the oldest architecture graduates in the country, so going to culinary school might be a better choice. It sounds like so much fun.

Sandra Malone

As director of Christian Counseling at Canaan Christian Church, you have a special relationship with your parishioners.
We have a very strong marriage counseling program and also offer family and grief counseling. So I am intimately involved with the congregation. Having that responsibility is heavy. It's hard to separate myself from their problems but I have to disconnect as much as possible and have learned to practice self-care.

You are also referred to as "First Lady" of the Canaan Christian Church. That's an impressive title.
In African American churches, the minister's wife is often referred to that way. I'm not really fond of that title because I don't like pedestals. I feel I'm a servant of God and want to be the best example of Christ that I can be. I just happen to be the wife of the pastor, but in God's eyes I'm like everyone else.

How important is faith in your life?
It *is* my life. I live, move, and have my being because of God. I rely on him for daily direction and guidance, and for inspiration when I need encouragement. I can always find strength through his word and spirit.

Do you ever question God?
I actually think it's healthy to question him and I don't think he's so fragile that we can't question him. But he has the right and authority to allow certain things. If I do ask him a question, I'm asking not out of anger or resentment, but am saying, "Lord, I don't fully understand why this had to happen, but I accept the fact that you are sovereign and I will still love you."

Do you think God is a man or a woman?
The Bible refers to God as a man, and I accept that. But he honors all of us the same. I don't feel that men are superior to women. The Bible teaches that the male has the role of being the head in the home and in a spiritual way to guide his family. And he is to love his wife like Christ loved the church.

How has the role of women in the church changed?
At Canaan, my husband, as pastor, has embraced and tried to promote women in the pulpit and having them have the same leadership responsibilities as men in the church.

What has been the biggest challenge in your life?
I went through a very difficult, earth-shattering time. It was a turning point. I came to know God in a whole new way. It was almost as if I could feel and touch him. I said, "Lord, you didn't send an angel; you came yourself to see about me." God blessed me to go back to school. I was terrified. The enemy had told me, and I think I had started to believe, that I was dumb and couldn't learn and excel. God put that to rest and gave me courage. For many semesters I had a 4.0 average. One semester I made a B and thought I was going to die. God sat me down on a bench and told me the journey was not about a degree, but that it was about learning to trust him. I knew he was not setting me up for failure. Later he guided me into marriage and family counseling.

The death of your parents was an especially difficult time for you, wasn't it?
Yes. They died six weeks apart. I was spiritually prepared but as a human being it was very hard. I want to believe that they have been able to see all the wonderful things that have happened, what they gave me, and what our family has been able to accomplish because of their hard work. I know they're in a great place and are just waiting.

How do you measure success?
By the number of lives you touch in an effort to make them better or be the most that they can be.

What's the best decision you have ever made?
Marrying my husband.

What do you like best about yourself?
That I don't have to have a crowd of people around me confirming that I'm okay. And, it isn't arrogance, but I really love myself.

And least?
Sometimes I have a problem asking for help because I feel like I have to do it all myself and don't want to weigh people down.

Is there anything people would be surprised to know about you?
I love going in the yard and digging in the dirt up to my elbows.

How do you feel about aging?
It's a gift. Everyone doesn't get the opportunity.

Staci Mandrola, M.D.

As a hospice and palliative care physician, you have the opportunity to get to know and to relate to a person in a profound way.
When I take care of someone who has a life-limiting illness, or is dying, the bullshit of usual human interactions falls away. I focus on what is important to that person in that moment. I get so much satisfaction figuring out what is important to them and helping them achieve those goals even though time is short. I have developed the ability to know when time is short and have a frank approach that allows me to say so. That's not true for many doctors because we're not taught in medical school how to deal with those situations.

Isn't your work terribly depressing?
I have sometimes felt overwhelmed, maybe overall emotional about certain patients or situations, but I've never felt depressed. There are so few people that do this work and so many people who need it. I've never had a patient or family say that what I did wasn't the most wonderful thing they've ever experienced. They're so grateful for the care they get, having someone hear them say what's important to them, and having treatment tailored to what their goal is for their medical care. Far too often, patients aren't asked what their goal is. We may assume it is to live as long as possible, but often that isn't it at all.

You become so involved with your patients. How do you not take that home with you?
Both my husband and I are physicians. A big part of what we talk about is our work lives. But I have made a conscious decision that I'm going to have time for work and time for home and family. It's a constant battle to keep that division between the two.

What, other than the people in your life, couldn't you live without?
Meditation and taking care of people who are dying have taught me that I can live without almost anything. You even learn from them that you can and do live without people you love. Millions of people do that every day. I scaled back running because of aches and pains, and I may have to scale back biking. I try not to be too attached to any of those things or material possessions because I know they can go away.

In a few words, how would you describe yourself?
Independent, self-motivated, compassionate.

What would you like to change about yourself?
I'd be more selfless. I do a lot of things for people but sometimes I wonder how much of it is for them and how much is for me.

If you weren't a doctor, what would you be doing?
I can't imagine not being a doctor. In a different life, I would work for Doctors Without Borders in whatever country had the most need.

What person of note would you most like to spend a day with?
The Dalai Lama---and my husband and famous medical blogger, John. He's my partner, buddy, and biggest supporter. It doesn't mean he doesn't annoy the crap out of me, sometimes. But when I have good news or something that's bothering me or something exciting, he's the first person I want to tell.

Why do you love biking so much?
It keeps me fit physically and mentally. I share it with my family and my team, Papa John's Racing Team. I do road, cyclocross and mountain biking. We are lucky to have gorgeous trails in the heart of the city. You get to be in nature, which my soul requires, and there are no cars to run over you!

Is there anything you regret?
The times when I was unkind.

What's your secret indulgence?
Dark chocolate, and the television series True Blood and Breaking Bad.

Do you think women or men make better friends?
It's not a question of better for me, just different. I will say men friends are less complicated. But, women friends who are mothers know my soul more.

What's next for you?
I went on a mission trip to Nicaragua and did maintenance work in an orphanage and daycare center. It was an amazing experience. I want to do that in other parts of the world. I became a grandma this past year, so Charlotte, my granddaughter, is a big part of my life. I can't wait to find out what "grandma" name she gives me.

Delanor Manson

You have said you experienced shocking discrimination while you were a student at the University of Kentucky.

I grew up in a cocoon in the African American community and was totally unaware of racism. I believed I could do anything. I was unprepared for the discrimination from both students and faculty at UK. I was told that people like me shouldn't be nurses and shouldn't get a bachelor's degree. My mother helped me understand that it wasn't my problem, but it was the problem of the people who believed that.

A career as an attorney got sidetracked and you became a nurse?

I wanted to be an attorney but got a scholarship to nursing school. When I became a nurse I realized that nurses weren't being cared for although they were the people who made care happen. My goal as a nurse was to take care of other nurses.

Being a Navy nurse took you around the world. You learned a lot about other people, especially the Japanese. And you discovered something interesting about Italian men.

I joined the Navy because I wanted to travel. I had amazing opportunities as a nurse to work in Japan, England, Germany, Italy, and Puerto Rico. I retired as a captain. I particularly enjoyed Japan because of the gentleness of the Japanese people and how they tried to include me in their culture even though I looked very different. It was in Japan that I took classes that spurred me on to being an artist. It was also where I became a devotee of Japanese food, especially sushi. I ate it three times a day, every day. It was my soul food.

I also loved living in Italy where I discovered that Italian men tend to be wild about brown women. I had no problem with that whatsoever. It felt really good.

Being a female officer in the Navy must have had its challenges.

Definitely. Some men were uncomfortable reporting to a woman. I had to convince them of my competency. I treated them with tremendous respect and allowed them some leeway to get to know me. If that didn't work, we resorted to the military way. I tried to show them that I possessed skills that would help us achieve our goals. When I retired there were so many people who made sure I understood that I had a tremendous, positive effect on their lives. I have had people tell me they are who they are today because of how I helped them grow.

How did you transition into being a jewelry designer?

It wasn't really a transition. I have always been fascinated by stones and their mysterious beauty. I started designing jewelry when I was very young. The pieces I made as a child were made of rope, wire, and rubber bands around rocks. I grew to be enchanted by the shape, color, and textures of stones, and I honed my talent as a designer. I have a very spiritual nature, and I think that is reflected in my work. I was thrilled to be able to open Koi Gallery to sell my work and share my love of jewelry with others.

What has been your most significant accomplishment?

I was Director of Quality for the Kentucky Cabinet for Health and Family Services. I was very involved in addressing how racism impacted children in the welfare system.

What do you like best about yourself?

That I eat healthy and that I exercise. And that I don't give up.

And least?

I don't give up. That can cause tremendous pain. I don't stop until I'm at the top of the mountain and have achieved what I set out to accomplish.

In a few words, how would you describe yourself?

Energetic, creative, focused, and caring.

Is there anything, other than the people in your life, you couldn't live without?

Sushi and a good glass of Chardonnay.

What's the most important thing you've learned about yourself?

That I can't do it all, no matter what. I always want to learn it all now and do it all now and be it all now. I want to take more art classes and learn more mediums, such as painting and sculpture, to be a more well-rounded artist. But I won't give up jewelry design because I think it's an art form for the soul.

Leigh Maroni

As a homicide detective with the Louisville Metro Police Department, you come face to face with brutality on a regular basis. Have you become immune to being shocked?

No, never. Just when you think you've seen it all, something new comes along. I have had to become somewhat desensitized to it but I still find myself shocked at some of the scenes I come upon. A lot of what I see involves gang wars. But when I see a real personal attack on someone outside of drug or gang culture, it can be more gruesome.

The police force has so many areas of specialization. Why did you choose homicide?

I had spent two years with Crimes Against Children. I realized I wanted to do more of an investigative, putting the puzzle together, whodunnit kind of thing, and the challenges that come along with that. And I feel that homicide, along with the abuse of a child, is the worst crime against humanity.

Isn't it frightening to respond to a call not knowing what you will encounter?

By the time Homicide is called out, the perimeter is usually set up by the first responding officers, and the threat has been removed.

How do you control your anger toward the possible perpetrators when you witness the aftermath of a heinous crime?

It's eventually my job to tell the story to a jury. But, if I let my emotions take over, it becomes my story. I need to be calm and in control and not let the situation control me. I have to be cognizant of what will happen down the road.

Few of us can resist a great police drama on television. You actually appeared in episodes of *The First 48* on A & E. What was that like?

It was demanding of my time. They wanted to follow us on every aspect of the cases. The public was going to see only one hour. It's hard to present 48 hours in one hour. And, it really put the pressure on us because we had a camera following us all the time. But it was exciting to represent the city and the department on television.

What would you be if you weren't a police officer?

I'd be in some aspect of social work. Maybe family therapy or something involved with children and the court system.

What motivates and inspires you?

My two children inspire me to be a good example for them.

What has been the most significant accomplishment in your life?

When I got on the department, my goal was to be a homicide detective. And I've done that. But, more importantly, I wanted to be a wife and mother. We weren't able to conceive, so we adopted a little girl. Then, by an act of God, we had a son. I want to spend as much time with my children but I also love my work.

Other than the people in your life, what couldn't you live without?

The sun. I love the growth and the sprouts of the spring and the warmth of the sun.

Is there anything that intimidates you?

No.

In three or four words, how would you describe yourself?

Honest, open, and funny.

What do you like best about yourself?

My dimples.

And least?

I can be very shy.

What's your biggest regret?

Not pushing myself athletically as much as I could have in high school.

What would people be surprised to know about you?

That I had a poem, *Peace Is*, published when I was a child.

That must have been a time when you were very idealistic. Have you changed your world view?

I don't think so. I have become more conservative because of my job, and I'm not very politically minded. But I very much believe in equality and fairness. At the same time, I don't believe in giving free handouts and not working. I think people should be held more responsible than they are.

Is there anything you would change about yourself if you could?

I'd be more outgoing and social.

You have a young daughter. What's the most important lesson you've learned that you will pass along to her?

That you can do anything you want to do in this world if you work hard enough for it.

Tori Murden McClure

You were the first woman to make a solo crossing of the Atlantic Ocean by rowboat, and were the first woman and first American to ski to the geographic South Pole. Yet you say you aren't an adventurer, but are an explorer.

There are two kinds of people who do endeavors like mine. Adventurers are chest-pounding thrill-seekers who climb the mountain and write about it, but explorers climb the mountain because they want to learn something about themselves. They can go where others have been and still explore. An adventurer would never go anywhere alone because there wouldn't be witnesses. I know explorers who never leave their desk. They just want to learn more, know more, and be more.

Was there a time during your 81 days at sea that you thought you wouldn't make it?

I was very prepared and had read everything about sailing across the ocean. There weren't many books about rowing, but I read them all. However, I didn't expect to get hit by Hurricane Daniel. I lost communications and then the Gulf Stream. Then the boat stopped. I capsized 11 times. I thought I was going to die but I wasn't going to have someone else die trying to help me.

Surely there were times that you were just plain bored.

It was a challenging time around high noon, when the sun was beating down, and the water was calm and flat.

Were there periods during the journey that you wished you hadn't embarked on it?

No, but there were times I wondered why I was doing it and times I thought I was an idiot.

In *A Pearl in the Storm*, you describe many of your experiences on the trip. Are there any you wish you had not been so honest about revealing?

Maybe I shouldn't have talked about throwing up every other chapter, or told about when in the midst of the hurricane I was in a dry suit and managed to heed nature's call in a zip-top bag. The bag flew out of my hand when the boat capsized, the bag broke, and the contents went all over my face.

You received a master's in divinity from Harvard, but went into the ordained ministry.

I went to the wrong divinity school. There were 60 people entering the class to get a degree to become a reverend. Only one got ordained. The school taught all the world's religions but sort of debunked your own sense of your own faith. That turned out to be good news for me. As a Presbyterian minister, there would be no way I would have been given the job of leading Spalding College, a Catholic institution. I'm still a very spiritual person, and my faith guides me.

Your perspective of feminism might surprise some people.

I went to Smith College. The feminism there is very different than at Harvard. The folks at Smith were prepared and trained, learned the necessary skills, and went into a job. At Harvard, it was more about people saying, "Poor me. I've been oppressed and abused." It's the victim mentality. There are people in the world who have chosen to make use of horrible things. Our stories aren't what happened to us, but what we do with them. I've never been comfortable playing the victim role more than 10 minutes. I find more opposition to who I am from women than from men. I think women are sometimes our own enemy. Women are the ones who ask why I row, why I climb mountains, as if what I do is wrong or bad. I feel as if they're telling me I'm stepping out of my boundaries and that I need to get back where I belong.

As president of Spalding University, you're not shy about bragging about the school.

Spalding is so much better than the perception of it. Part of that conception has to do with the social stereotype of it once having been a women's college. Bellarmine had educated men and Spalding had educated women. People thought Bellarmine must be better. We formerly were run by nuns. It wouldn't have occurred to them to brag. It's now time to brag a little.

What keeps you awake at night?

I'm not worried about Spalding versus any other school, but I worry about the students I can't save, the ones who are too far to reach because of personal situations. I know I can't save the world. I don't notice the victories so much, but I notice the losses. If I let the victories go to my head, I'd be even more insufferable than I am sometimes.

Catherine McCord

Your history is star-studded, from fashion runway to the big screen. Start at the beginning!

A friend signed me up to be a model for the former Lazarus store in Louisville. After that I won the Louisville title in the Look of the Year contest, sponsored by Elite modeling agency, and competed in Japan. I received "Best Personality" but didn't place. Elite signed me during high school. I lived in Paris and New York while I was a teenager. In my senior year of high school I was discovered by Calvin Klein. At that time it was a very big deal.

Give us the inside scoop on some of the top designers.

Calvin Klein is lovely, and Donna Karan is hilarious. She's the best, full of life and energy.

Runway models never look like they're having fun. Why do they look bored or in pain?

It's about the clothes, not the model.

You've been on the covers of *Glamour*, *Elle*, *Brides* and Italian *Vogue*, and have appeared in the Victoria Secret catalog. Those must be heady experiences.

It's always surreal. For me, it's more about getting the job, not so much the vanity thing.

But you weren't content with modeling?

I started working for the television program *Extra* as a reporter. I knew it would help me get into television hosting, something I had always wanted to do. I've also appeared in some films. It's all rather exciting, I must admit.

All during that time food was a true love.

I grew up with a huge interest in food. My grandparents and cousins and I would go to the you-pick farms, and my grandparents had a wonderful garden. Food was such an integral part of our lives. Later, I got to go to cool places and eat cuisine around the world when I was modeling. I had always had a fantasy of going to culinary school. Finally I did that, acting and hosting during the day and attending culinary school at night. I worked in restaurants and for catering companies but decided 16 hours on the line wasn't for me.

I've forever been an advocate of farmers' markets; probably 80 percent of the food my family and I eat now is from the markets. I have always loved cooking and cookbooks but realized I didn't know how to cook for a baby when my son was born. I started pureeing fruits and vegetables, and started blogging about it.

Your Web site, weelicious.com, has become a hot spot.

It encompasses recipes and a great deal of information about fast, easy, and fresh cooking. We have about 1.4 million unique visitors a month.

And you have books in the works?

I'm writing two books; one focuses on getting children to be good eaters from day one. It is 30 percent information and 70 percent recipes. The second book is about 180 days of school lunches.

As a model, actor, and television personality, much of the emphasis has been on your appearance. How are you dealing with aging and how it changes your look?

I'm good with it. I spent so many years looking into the mirror. I love that it's no longer about that. It was bizarre to have my life be all about the outside. Now it's the polar opposite.

What's the best decision you ever made?

There isn't just one. There are three. First would be that I saved the money I made modeling so I could do what I wanted with my life. Second would be going to culinary school. The other great decision was home-birthing my daughter. I had my son at the hospital; it was a long, drawn-out process. When I was six months pregnant with my daughter, I watched *The Business of Being Born*, a documentary made by some friends. I said, "I can do that." Having her at home was a very empowering, life-changing experience.

What do you like best about yourself?

I move fast and am a multitasker. I also like that I am easy-going and can get along with most people.

And least?

I put a lot of pressure on myself. I'm very driven.

Who are the most fascinating women you know or know about?

Alice Waters, the chef, restaurateur and food activist. At this time in my life, I'm also fascinated by Michelle Obama and her platform of healthy living and gardening.

What one thing would you change about yourself if you could?

Nothing, because then I wouldn't be me.

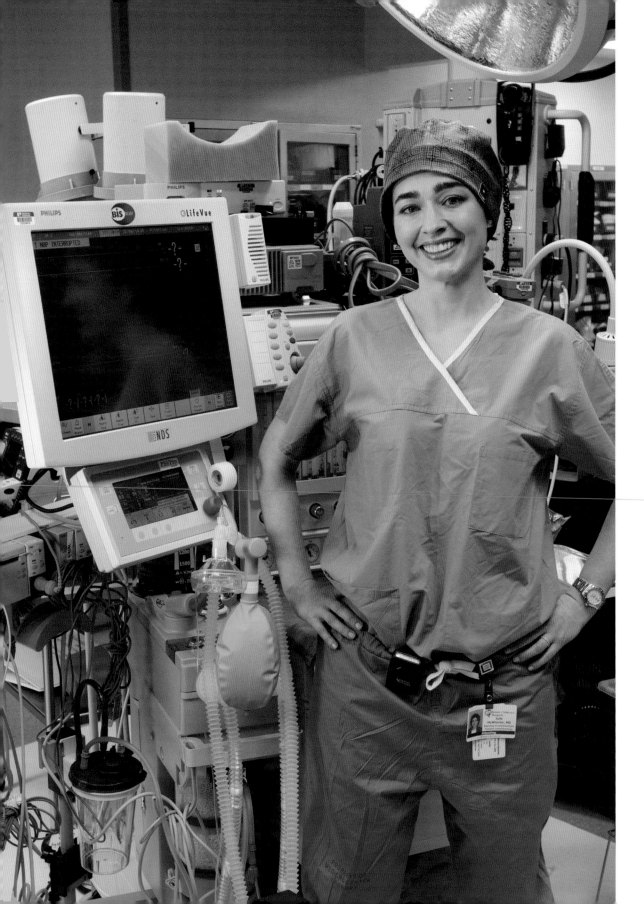

Julie McWhorter, M.D.

Why did you choose the specialty of congenital cardiac anesthesiology?
I love children. It's so challenging to work with children who are critically ill and have cardiac defects. Quite a few of them have repairs done in stages and will often come back for follow-ups. Medical progress in the last 20 or 30 years has enabled children with congenital cardiac defects to grow into adulthood. It's a very exciting area to be involved in.

Your medical mission trip to Ecuador was very special to you.
Seventeen physicians from the Louisville area went to Ecuador with Heal the Children. We performed approximately 150 pediatric surgeries of all kinds in a week's time. We took all of our own supplies, and had to operate under very poor conditions with limited supplies and resources. The trip was a wonderful experience. I was moved by the pride of the Ecuadorian doctors, nurses, and patients and their families. I was particularly impressed by an Ecuadorian medical student who donated his time and helped plan with our group. He is completing medical school in Ecuador and will apply for a surgical residency at U of L. It's a difficult position to be in, but I always champion the underdog. As a woman, I know what it's like to be in not the most opportune position.

You've said you are very ambitious.
I'm not sure where that ambition will take me in medicine. I have started to lecture on a national level, so I plan on being in the forefront of my field. I'm excited about applying for some MBA programs. I want to pursue business opportunities in the community and help my pediatric anesthesia group to be profitable and sustainable in the future. And, I may pursue entrepreneurial opportunities as they arise.

You met your husband on eHarmony?
It was difficult to meet people because of the amount of time I spend working. I went on eHarmony and he was the first person I met. I said I was adventurous and outgoing and was looking for someone like that. I also liked him because he's a major in the Army, and has a great deal of compassion and integrity. On our first date we went to the stock car races and Maker's Mark Distillery. Right away I knew he was special. After being together a year, we eloped to Savannah.

You've said your husband is married to the military.
He's third generation military. He loves the Army. It gives him such a sense of purpose. He has been to Bosnia, Korea, and Iraq. This is his first deployment since we've been together. I feel honored to be married to him and I'm proud that he serves our country.

Is there anything people would be surprised to know about you?
I've been told by people at work that I'm very focused on completing a task, so they don't realize until they meet me outside work or in a social situation that I'm very adventurous and energetic.

How would you describe yourself?
Adventurous, ambitious, passionate, and approachable. I'm passionate about my patients and the work I do, and about my friends and family. I live life to the fullest.

How do you like to spend your spare time?
I love to salsa dance. I also like to mountain bike. I have a map of the United States on a wall. I plan to ride my mountain bike in every state. I have about 15 down so far, including Alaska and Hawaii. I'm a certified scuba diver, but I don't get to do that much. I also do a bit of trail running.

What would you be if you weren't a physician?
A music producer.

What haven't you done that you'd like to do?
I want to go on more medical mission trips. Where I go doesn't really matter to me. There are plenty of people to be helped almost everywhere in the world.

How do you feel about aging?
Beauty is only skin deep. Aging is inevitable so you need to be an interesting person underneath. Botox and plastic surgery? I haven't done them yet but I wouldn't be opposed to them.

Is there one woman you find particularly fascinating?
Elizabeth Taylor was my idol. She said she wanted her tombstone to read, "She lived." She really did live. The love story between her and Richard Burton was so wonderful. I believe she said they may have loved each other too much.

Do you think you love your husband too much?
I think I love him just enough.

Angela Merrick

You're a detective with the Louisville Metro Police Department. What inspired you to become a police officer?
While studying accounting in college, I realized it wasn't the career for me. A personality test revealed that I was suited for law enforcement. Not long after, I knew I would enjoy it because I like helping people and being active in the community. It has been everything I had hoped for, and more.

Have you experienced much sexism as a police officer?
When I was new with the force, I noticed that people would often look more to my male counterpart and would sometimes talk down to me. But as long as I took care of the situation, it became obvious I would do my job. I used to run into other officers who were old-school and didn't feel women should be in the field. That has changed over the years. Also, I have gained the respect of my male co-workers. They know I will be there to back them up.

Does your life in the police department in any way resemble television shows such as *Law and Order*?
I watch those shows and kind of laugh and think, wow, I wish I could wrap up my cases or get the DNA back that fast. Those types of shows can hinder our cases because the public may not understand that television doesn't portray reality. However, some of the newer crime shows are presenting more realistic scenarios.

Early on in your career you encountered a considerable amount of risk.
I had to do my time on the streets. I worked in the Narcotics division for six months. That was enough time to convince me that Narcotics wasn't worth my life. Things could have become ugly very fast. For a time, I was on a crisis intervention team and was also a hostage negotiator. I loved that but stopped that work when I became pregnant. Of course, in my present job, there is always a risk. And I have to constantly think ahead in a tactical manner and be prepared for the worst.

Now, as a member of the Child Protective Division, you investigate child sexual and physical abuse. You're dealing with horrific crimes.
Unlike the revolving door for criminals that I had previously had to deal with, this division puts people away so that they don't have a chance to repeat their crimes. It's more rewarding than any past assignments. I do have to put my emotions in check and it takes a lot of patience. I have learned to be very cordial with the accused and earn their trust in order to get admissions and confessions.

Are you able to separate your work from being the mother of a small child?
Seeing what I see and working these cases definitely makes me more protective of my son, and probably more paranoid.

What has been the biggest challenge in your life?
Dealing with my separation and fighting for custody of my child. I used to think that graduating college and joining the police force were the best things I could ever do. Then I had my son and realized that he is so much more important than anything else.

Other than the people in your life, what couldn't you live without?
My gun. I always feel safe knowing I have it.

How would you describe yourself?
Strong, level-headed, laid-back, and patient.

What has been the most defining moment in your life?
The birth of my son. From that I learned a lot about myself. It brought up a lot of old family issues that I didn't want to bring into his life.

What do you like best about yourself?
I'm a strong, secure person.

What would people be surprised to know about you?
That I'm an emotional person. But it isn't evident on the job because I have to be professional.

Do you have any regrets?
My main regret is being confrontational with my ex.

What traits do you most like in a person?
Friendliness and confidence.

And least?
I don't like people who are controlling or overbearing.

How do you measure success?
By how happy and positive people are in their lives and how secure and confident they are about themselves. You really have to be happy with and love yourself.

Susan Moloney

You have such an obvious passion for your career as an interior designer.
It's such a wonderful artistic outlet. My mother, daughter, and lots of cousins are artists, and my sister is a jewelry designer, so I think I've come by it naturally. It's exciting and fulfilling to visualize what to do with a space. I enjoy interpreting a client's taste and taking it to another level. I have strong opinions about how rooms are used and how people live in them.

Being a designer isn't all fun. Ten percent is fun and 90 percent is hard work. Another designer told me a long time ago that after 20 years I wouldn't be so creative, but I haven't become that callous or feel like it's not worth the extra effort. My children think I'm possessed.

What would you like to do if you weren't a designer?
I'd be an architect or a painter. There has never been a convenient time for me to go to school to be an architect. Painting is the same way. You have to commit to it, and I don't like to do anything mediocre. But every once in a while I go on a tangent and paint.

Is there a difference between taste and style?
Style is personal. Taste is something everyone has, no matter what the level. When I think of style, I think of star quality. Trends come and go, but if they don't fit you or your lifestyle, they're not something you should follow. Although I don't want a room to ever scream a time period, there are some things that are classic. I think there's a pulse in design, but it doesn't mean you have to take it to the outer limits.

How do you deal with clients who have…well, bad taste?
I don't like to hurt people's feelings but I have suggested that certain things would look good in the basement! People pay me to tell them what I think. I hope I'm diplomatic about it. Sometimes I have to work around things that are just dreadful. But there are times that I have to eat my words when I find that a piece works well even though I thought it was awful.

What inspires you?
Traveling and reading and shopping. My children influence me to some degree. My daughter is in the art world in New York. I've become friends with many of the artists, and they definitely inspire me.

Do you ever run out of ideas?
I have highs and lows, periods in which I'm more creative than others. I try to do things to make myself be creative. If I'm feeling down, I exercise, read a novel, or look through books of some of my favorite designers over the years. Movies are a kind of escapism for me and can bring back my creativity. A change of pace keeps my creative juices flowing. I like to go to Key West where the pace is much slower.

What's the best decision you have made?
I made a turning point about 10 years ago. I put more emphasis on my career. I think that was a very good decision for me, personally, and for my children. I'm doing what I love.

Other than the people in your life, what couldn't you live without?
My sunglasses and my iPhone.

What do you like best about yourself?
I think I did a good job with my children.

And least?
Photographs of myself.

Is there anything you'd change about yourself if you could?
I'd be less compulsive.

What's your biggest regret?
I make a point of not regretting; it's a waste of precious time.

How are you handling aging?
It's surprising to me, as a female, that the older I've gotten, the happier I've become. I knew my grandmother when she was my age. She seemed so very old to me, but I don't feel old at all. I am more confident in myself. I like the age I am and where I am in my life and living in my own skin.

Who is the most fascinating woman you know or know about?
My mother. She's terribly creative and has paved the way for me to be the free spirit I am. I also like strong women in history. Cleopatra and Queen Elizabeth I immediately come to mind.

Mary Moseley

Were you surprised when your father tapped you to take over his business, the Al J. Schneider Company, which includes office buildings, The Galt House, Crowne Plaza, and a building supply business?

I was shocked, as were members of my family. But no one disputed his choice because none of us ever questioned him about his decisions. Why he selected me instead of one of my siblings, I'll never know. I had not been in the business. The day after he died, I got a call from one of the workers saying, "Where do you want me to go today?" I had no clue so I asked him where he usually went. After he told me, I said, "Go there today and we'll talk tomorrow." Dad had asked several of his closest advisors, wise men from all walks of life, to cover my back. They mentored me through my first several years.

You made major changes in The Galt House. Why?

Former Mayor Armstrong would tell Dad that The Galt House was bringing down the city of Louisville because the property was deteriorating. Dad thought it was in great shape. He was a very conservative fellow. As a family, we hadn't done anything to improve it out of respect for him. After he died, we had to completely renovate the hotel. He would be flipping to know that we borrowed so much money. But he would be happy that the city is proud of The Galt House.

Do you feel that you have to live up to him or that you are in his shadow?

I never could live up to him and don't try to. He was a remarkable person. I wish I had a tenth of his vision.

What's your biggest challenge?

Getting things done in the city. There's a world of committees to go through for approvals. Papers sit on people's desks for weeks, slowing progress.

As a woman, were you not respected or taken seriously?

My mentors were wonderful. I did have problems with some of the people I do business with, and some employees. I had to earn their respect, and I feel that I have earned it.

You seem like a very determined person.

I love my team. I encourage their input on going forward and want to know the changes they'd like to make. Once we make a decision, I stay the course and am very focused. When the plan is in place, I hold everyone accountable.

Of what accomplishments are you most proud?

My children. Although the world has so many outside temptations and influences, they turned out to be respectful, independent, community-oriented adults. I love them. I'm also proud of getting through a $60 million renovation of The Galt House. Its grandeur was restored. It wasn't easy getting the family to approve that much borrowed money, and the logistics of removing and replacing 1,300 rooms of carpet, wallpaper, and furniture, and upgrading public spaces were very challenging. It was my first experience jumping into such a large project. I feel really good about it.

Is there anything people would be surprised to know about you?

I came in third place in the Miss America Model Pageant in Grossinger, New York, when I was the young age of 18.

What haven't you done that you would like to do?

I'd like to have the time to paint portraits, something I used to do. I'd also like to travel more. I want to see the pyramids and architecture of Egypt.

What do you like best about yourself?

I'm very trustworthy. My word is as good as a handshake or a signed piece of paper. Dad was the same way.

Do you have a major regret?

That I was not given more children. I was given three; one was taken away at birth. That was not in our hands.

What would you do if you weren't president of the company?

I'd like to do volunteer work with children and to spend more time with my grandchild (and someday more grandchildren). I'd also do more tinkering around the house. I like having a hammer in my hand.

Who's the most fascinating woman you know or know about?

Nancy Reagan. She's intelligent and charming. She so elegantly stepped into the role of First Lady. I loved how she and Ronald interacted through their letters. She had a very tough side, but also a very soft side.

Mary Margaret Mulvihill

It didn't come as a surprise to anyone that you entered politics.

Growing up in an Irish Catholic Democrat family, there were constant discussions of issues and politics. I was a precinct captain in the party by the time I was in high school. My aunt and I went to JFK's inaugural. It was inspiring and wonderful. That was kind of the beginning for me. When Harvey Sloane ran for mayor I worked in his campaign. Then I ran for the Board of Aldermen and won, and served three terms. It was tough from the get-go because William Stansbury was mayor and we didn't see eye-to-eye. A group of us tried to impeach him but that went nowhere. Later, I was named director of Neighborhoods, which was a great job. It was really where the action was. With 120 neighborhoods in Louisville, it was very exciting. But I loved being the administrator of Human Services because I could see the profound difference we were making in people's lives. Throughout all that time there was a core group of people trying to help those who were less fortunate. We felt like we could win any war. I don't know if that could ever happen again.

You get upset when you talk about the vitriol that seems to have taken over politics.

I have never seen such ugliness, especially on the national scene. It makes me so sad to see all the energies directed to fighting when they could be directed to serving the better good.

As a member of the TARC board of directors, do you think Louisvillians will ever really embrace public transportation?

Unless they're very involved with environmental issues or can't afford gas, probably not. Most people just don't want to be inconvenienced. But I believe a viable transit system is imperative if we're to have a good city.

Do you have any Republican friends?

No, not really. I know there are some nice Republicans, but I'm so ingrained in the Democratic Party that my friends happen to share my views. The parties have vastly different values. All of the important social programs have come out of the Democratic Party.

You're a supporter of Kentucky Citizens Against the Death Penalty. Are there any circumstances for which you would support the death penalty?

Under no circumstances. I think that should be up to God. We have the mechanism to severely punish people for their crimes, to put them in prison for life to think about the crimes they committed. I can think of no worse horror than to sit in a cell and know that the doors to the prison will never open. To me, that seems to be a sentence far worse than death.

Are you positive about the future?

The world has changed and is now more troubled than ever before. There's upheaval everywhere, and we're slowly destroying the Earth. Everything seems very complex and, in some cases, dire. I hope things will be brighter for my grandchildren, but I just don't know.

Friendships are central to your life, aren't they?

I treasure friendship. I have so many friends, mostly female, who make my life full and happy. Do women make better friends than men? Absolutely. I can't imagine a woman without a friend but I don't think it is as important to men. My husband says he can't believe I stay on the phone for an hour talking to a female friend and basically say nothing. But it's not really nothing. We talk out things and tell stories.

What has been the defining moment in your life?

My son was married to a most wonderful woman who died at 29. It had such an impact on all our lives. Something like that changes you dramatically, in some ways positively. You start looking at what has meaning in life; the little things don't seem as important.

Have you "found" yourself?

Yes, no question about it.

Who's the most fascinating woman you know or know about?

Frances Perkins, U.S. Secretary of Labor under FDR, and one of the orchestrators of the New Deal. She was a phenomenal woman. I never felt she got credit for the New Deal. I love her life.

How do you feel about aging?

I don't mind growing old. In some ways, it's a beautiful time because you have more time to spend on things you really like, and you're much wiser. Would I want to be 20 again? No. I think 45 would be a good age at which to stay. That's kind of when everything is clicking.

Renee Murphy

Sports reporting was originally your goal. Now you're a news anchor at WHAS. What happened in between?

I was always an athlete while growing up. I saw Robin Roberts, now on *Good Morning America*, when she was on ESPN. I thought her job looked like fun. After majoring in broadcast journalism at Virginia Commonwealth University, I got a job at ESPN as a production assistant. Three hundred other 22-year-old people and I worked long hours running around like chickens with our heads cut off. It was much more intense than I was prepared for at 22, but I loved it and it prepared me for the next step.

I had sent out tons of resume tapes that showed my sports reporting and anchoring. I received a call from a little station in Mississippi offering me a job in news. I told them I was adamant about sports. They agreed that I would anchor the weekend news and also do the Friday night football show. I took the job thinking it would be worth it to get on the air. I ended up liking news and having the ability to tell a variety of stories. I moved on to Youngstown, Ohio, and then came to Louisville.

Television is a very cutthroat, competitive business. Do you worry that at any given time you could be replaced?

Anything can happen any day. That's the nature of the beast. I enjoy it so much I can't worry about what will happen tomorrow or next year.

You've covered such a wide variety of stories. What has been one of the most memorable?

One of my most interesting interviews was with a teacher at Valley High School who used the "n" word with his students. He was very honest with me and admitted he didn't understand why some people could use the word and he couldn't. When the interview was concluded, the photographer and I couldn't even speak for a minute, then looked at each other and said, "Did that really happen?" The reaction and feedback after the story ran was incredible.

How do you remain stoic and professional when covering difficult stories?

We've covered tons of horrific and tragic events. The murders of children are probably the most difficult to cover. But for any difficult story, I have to put my guard up and disconnect myself from the story. It becomes an almost out-of-body experience. It isn't until I get home or am with friends that I can let my guard down about it.

Viewers often think working in television must be very glamorous.

Local news is very fast-paced and not glamorous. They don't see us running around the newsroom in our flip flops or rushing to put on eyeliner before we go on the air. I've been asked if I have someone to do my makeup. I'm that person.

What's next for you professionally?

In the next five years I'd like to still be anchoring and reporting. I hope it's in Louisville, but if not, I hope to be doing the same thing and same quality of work wherever I am.

Describe your ideal day off.

If the kids are away for the weekend and I have a day to escape, I like to go to a movie, do a couple of scrapbook pages, read part of a good book, and have a great dinner. I wouldn't cook. I would go out. Otherwise I wouldn't consider it a great dinner.

What's the best decision you've ever made?

Marrying my high school sweetheart. He has been my biggest cheerleader and has given me the courage to pursue my dream of broadcasting. Had I not met him I'm not sure I would have gone for it as aggressively as I did.

What do you like best about yourself?

For the most part, I'm pretty even keeled. It takes a lot to send me over the edge. Maybe badgering and pestering, or a multitude of things happening at the same time would do it.

And least?

Because I'm compassionate, I can be a pushover. I'd like to take up for myself more.

Who's the most fascinating woman you know?

My mother. She's a strong woman and has done what she wanted to do. She has had challenges but has come out with grace and dignity and has followed her heart.

With which person of note would you most like to spend the day?

Oprah, because she's accomplished far more than she ever imagined. So many people depend on her for their livelihood. With great power comes great responsibility.

Sena Jeter Naslund

You are the nationally acclaimed author of *Adam and Eve*, *Abundance*, *Four Spirits*, *Ahab's Wife*, and *Sherlock in Love*, in addition to two collections of stories: *The Disobedience of Water* and *Ice Skating at the North Pole*. What influences and inspires you?

I'm inspired by history, for sure. But my career started with being a frustrated musician. Nearly all my short stories celebrated the art of music. More recently I celebrate the visual arts. Also, the Civil Rights Movement and antiwar/antiviolence are repeatedly referred to in my writing.

Do you try to separate yourself from your characters and story line?

I try to create convincing worlds in my fiction. I want to transport the reader from one time and place to another time and place. My views of life are necessary and should come through. But I don't regard myself as writing propagandist literature.

Is one of your novels your favorite?

I don't think so. It's sort of like a parent's relationship with children. At times you can see the good points of one over the other but you love them all.

But some of your characters are far from lovable.

Sometimes I write about characters that aren't very admirable. Ryder Jones in *Four Spirits* is a Ku Klux Klan member. I didn't like imagining myself inside of him, but after many efforts I recognized that despite all his terrible ideas and emotions, he, too, was a human being. I try to realize we're all flawed human beings. My characters are not flawless. They all need to learn and grow.

Prior to becoming a successful author, did you receive stacks of rejection letters?

Certainly. I tried to learn when people were kind enough to say why they rejected the piece. Once I was having trouble publishing my short stories in individual journals. I was writing things that interested me and a small group of people but they weren't getting published much. I asked myself what was being published. I read contemporary literary journals and concluded that most of the stories had in common a zany voice. I said, "Okay, I can write in a zany voice." I was mad, but I did it. As I was writing, first out of anger, I got interested in the new directions the new voice was taking me. I sent a piece that was rejected by two small literary magazines. I read a story in the *Paris Review* that I thought was a lot like mine, only mine was better. I sent mine to the *Paris Review*. Within two weeks, I got a personal letter from George Plimpton saying he wanted to publish *The Animal Way to Love*. I had discovered a whole new

territory to explore. I advise anyone having trouble getting published to read contemporary literature that is being published to determine what publishers like. It's not selling out, but expanding your horizons.

You were outraged when you read a *Courier-Journal* headline, "Yoga can be Dangerous to Christians." It was written by Albert Mohler, president of the Southern Baptist Theological Seminary in Louisville.

In his blog, Mohler wrote, "Christians are not called to empty the mind or to see the human body as a means of connecting to and coming to know the divine." According to the *C-J*, Mohler sees yoga as so interwoven with Eastern mysticism that it is "at odds with the Christian understanding." I was appalled. Why should we define ourselves as narrowly as possible? That's going in the wrong direction. We should be open to as many enriching experiences of the body, mind, and soul as we can.

You are Writer in Residence at the University of Louisville, and program director of the Spalding University brief-residency MFA in Writing. Can good writing be taught if the person isn't creative?

Many people love to say creative writing cannot be taught. I don't believe that.

Do you ever suffer from writer's block?

Never. And I've never met the student I couldn't cure of writer's block.

Can writing be painful?

Sometimes. It's also very joyful sometimes.

Are you worried that electronic books will lead to the demise of great bookstores?

Television didn't end radio; it just let radio do what it does best. I'm technologically challenged. I will probably read some electronic books, but I do love the book as an artifact.

What's the most important thing you've learned about yourself?

When I was a girl, my mother said, and my character Una, in *Ahab's Wife*, said, "Be brave." I still have to tell myself to be brave. I think you have to be brave to get through life.

Janey Newton

You were a pioneer in that you introduced a different philosophy of education to Louisville.

As a new teacher at St. Francis, I devised my own curriculum for primary grades. It was based on a Waldorf education, designed by Rudolph Steiner. It integrates practical, artistic, and conceptual elements, and emphasizes the role of imagination in learning. At the time, no one grasped what I was doing; they only knew I was getting good results. I left St. Francis and went to the Rudolph Steiner College in California and became even more intrigued by his approach. I brought it back to the Meredith Dunn Learning Center and applied it to children who have learning disabilities. It worked again. While there I created the Curriculum Resource Center, a place where teachers could get inspired about how to bring hands-on learning to their classroom, and to use the arts in math, science, and history. That is solidly a Waldorf education. Later I was asked to join the Gheens Academy and infused it with Rudolph Steiner's ideas of child development. The next step for me was to start a Waldorf School. Starting a school was an amazing project. I learned so much about myself, how an organization works, and how to make progress and not get stuck.

Foxhollow Farm, of which you are an owner, is a sustainable and biodynamic farm community. It began as a much different concept.

My mother had started an alternative health clinic and spa, with a bed and breakfast. She was developing Alzheimer's disease. On one level she understood her situation, but not intellectually. She asked me to help with Foxhollow. Alternative medicine wasn't supported at the time and the business couldn't survive financially. We waited until she wasn't aware of what was happening before we closed it. It was terribly sad but so many people had been helped.

We were left with 1,300 acres and an empty building. My brother, sister, and I decided to create a biodynamic farm, which is based on Rudolph Steiner's foundation of agriculture. The land had been chemically treated and commercially farmed for 35 years, so different from our vision of health. We went cold turkey, no more chemicals. Consultants told us we needed cows on the land to bring health and fertility to the soil. That led to our grass-fed beef. We then started a CSA, Community Supported Agriculture, which is kind of like a vegetable club in which members get a weekly box of harvested vegetables. After that, we expanded into a large market garden, then a farm store. We also sell local chicken, pork, and lamb. The freshest meat and vegetables are available at Foxhollow all year. I turned the former clinic into an education center where we conduct cooking classes and art classes, and workshops on topics such as gardening, biodynamics, and beekeeping.

Is it intended to be a money-making venture?

I hope to show people that a biodynamic method can be used and still make money. However, we don't consider it a profit center. It's a labor of love that we hope will be sustainable. It's getting there.

You must be an expert gardener.

Are you kidding? I can't grow anything. Even my houseplants die. My gift is teaching and facilitating, not growing the food.

What's the best decision you ever made?

To start each morning either meditating or thoughtfully journaling, to be really centered. I tune in to the part of me that is wiser than the frantic, busy bee part.

With which person of note would you most like to spend the day?

The Dalai Lama. I feel that he has reached the place where he has such trust in the divine flow. He's so filled with joy because of his trust.

What haven't you done that you would like to do?

I want to explore. I'm intrigued by the idea of leadership that has a more feminine, nurturing quality. It's about leading within a circle rather than leading from the top down. But it is a quality of strength, not all mushy-huggy. It's not a leadership style that applies only to women. I also want to do more teaching about Steiner's philosophy and to help people face their challenges through art and talking and philosophy. One thing that helps me is to believe that things we consider bad happening in the physical world actually have a higher purpose. It's easier to overcome obstacles if you know there are jewels later.

Anne Northup

You represented Kentucky's third Congressional district in the U.S. House of Representatives and were a member of the House Appropriations Committee. You wielded considerable power and influence in Washington. But you were also a very involved mother to your children. How did you balance your two lives?

My Congressional career was never the sum total of my life. I was one of 10 children and I always wanted a big family. Woody and I married 42 years ago and had six children. I've always seen myself as wife, mom, daughter, and sister.

Don't you think politics have become increasingly partisan and the politicians increasingly vitriolic?

Not really. I had great friends when I was a member of the Kentucky House of Representatives. My best mentors in the State House were across the aisle. There were so many Democrats who were pro-growth and had the same perspectives I did. In Washington, it was shocking, I don't mind saying. I was in the majority, but not a large majority. I felt like everything the Democrats did every day was about how they could get back in the majority. Of course, there is a lot of passion about issues. How can anyone not get passionate about important issues that impact our country? I don't mind vigorous debates or the fact that people have beliefs that are the polar opposite of mine. Hearing different viewpoints is why we have campaigns. But it bothers me very much when facts are denied for the purpose of winning a campaign.

Winning an election must be as exciting as losing one is crushing.

Losing something you had is harder than losing something you didn't have. I don't think I felt the loss of my Congressional district because my son Joshua had recently died. I was numb from his death. I felt like I couldn't get up from the kitchen table, but my kids couldn't get out of bed. Woody said we need to pattern the behavior of our kids. We didn't want Josh's death to define their lives. Our daughter got married a few months later. Our whole family was determined to pull together.

What affected me about losing my Congressional seat was the loss of relationships with people I had worked closely beside, and my involvement with this community. There was a huge emptiness.

You don't mince words when it comes to the press and local politics.

Certain things have let this community down, and nothing more so than *The Courier-Journal*. The paper has a blind addiction to policies that it has held on to forever. The editorial board refuses to look at facts and has terribly abused its power.

It's ironic that in Louisville you're considered legitimate only if you're a Democrat, especially a liberal Democrat. There is an enormous effort to sideline other thinking. The press and city leadership acted as if they had the Ten Commandments of how to run the city. The strongest group that stood up to them was the African American community and the pastors of those churches. But the political leadership of the churches continued the policies of victimization. Contrarily, the pastors were asking about what we should do with education, health, safety of children, and housing for the elderly. They were looking for solutions. They got quite a pushover from their own organizations for working with me. The pastors couldn't be controlled or owned by the leadership of the churches. Greater Louisville Inc. (GLI) is always an arm of the mayor. That's not true of the Chamber of Commerce in most cities.

Do you think of yourself as a feminist?

I'm from a family of 10 girls. We all did well in school, competed athletically, and were expected to be responsible. I define feminism as women making their own way, just the same as men. Obviously, I've done that. Unfortunately, in many circles you're not considered a real woman if you're not liberal. Many women say they're promoting the best interest of women, but they're really promoting their own liberal agendas. They don't want anyone different than them to be on the move. They don't allow open debate.

You're now commissioner of the Consumer Product Safety Commission.

It would be tedious to many people, but I've never been so closely involved with administrative law, and I enjoy that.

You're very positive about Republican women in office today.

When I was in Congress there weren't a lot of Republican women. And the ones who had seniority were moderates and usually sided with the Democrats. Today there's a whole group of Republican women who are smart, articulate, and conservative. They're interested in a wide array of issues, not only those that are considered traditional women's issues.

Ann Oldfather

You're one of the most prominent plaintiffs' attorneys in Louisville, and continually rank at the top of the best lawyers lists.
What has made you so successful?

I suppose more than anything is the fact that I get to do something I love. And there's something fundamental in me that wants to help. The law is a marvelous challenge and a wonderful way to help. A person's money, influence and power don't give them an advantage in a courtroom. In front of a jury, it's a level playing field. A jury cares about who they believe and who has the moral high ground.

Isn't it a bit of theater?

Yes, to some degree. Something surprising always happens and there can be dramatic moments of truth. I'm responsible for communicating a story that's often very complicated. But I don't have the freedom of a screenwriter. I can't make things up.

Your reputation is that of being brutal. Is it justified?

When prospective clients tell me they want a brutal attorney, I explain that's not what they want. They really want someone who will be their fierce advocate. I am a zealous advocate for my clients. I think I'm tough. And I really don't care whether people like me or not when I am sticking up for you. What people think of me in terms of taking care of my clients can't cause me to back off to try to please the other attorney or judge.

I know I'm direct and to the point, but I'm still trying to learn that people perceive me differently than I perceive myself. A *Courier-Journal* article about me had the headline, "Brilliant and Brash." That "brash" part was a little painful---and the brilliant was overstated. I don't think I'm brash, but I can see how other people might.

Would you dread being your opposing attorney?

No. I'd enjoy it.

Do you have a soft side?

If you know me only in the courtroom, you have no idea who I am. I cry at movies and pick up stray cats.

When you began practicing law in a large firm, did you experience much discrimination from prospective clients, judges and other lawyers?

Yes to all of those. Every now and then, we worked with the stodgy establishment type. Some clients and partners were reluctant to have me on certain cases. Eventually I was the first woman to be made partner. But I realized I wasn't satisfied and left to "do my own thing." It wasn't all negative by any means. I loved that firm and they gave me wonderful opportunities.

What would you be if you weren't an attorney?

So many things. A doctor. A painter. An actress. A writer. We'd live on a farm and have 11 children. I'd can my own vegetables.

What has been the biggest challenge of your life?

Dealing with the reality of having only 24 hours in a day. That leads to questions of balance…who do you give your time to and what are your own expectations about the kind of job you're going to do.

And your major disappointment?

Discovering that some high profile, well-placed lawyers are not ethical and that there are other lawyers, their friends, who don't care. Friendships can never trump our obligation to tell the truth. Maybe I need to be more cynical, but I still find that profoundly disappointing.

Other than the people in your life, what couldn't you live without?

A challenge of some kind.

Is there anything that intimidates you?

My husband. He has very high standards and I am sure that I constantly disappoint him. Also, it concerns me that people in my personal life think because my professional life is so important to me that I put it above my relationships with them.

What's the best decision you ever made?

To take a flier and go to law school.

What would people be surprised to know about you?

That my forms of escape are painting, movies and books.

Is there anything you'd like to change about yourself?

That I'll get to the gym every single day.

Finish the sentence, "I wish women would…

remember that feminism is not a dirty word." The generation after us seems to feel it must repudiate feminism. When a woman says she isn't a feminist, I always want to say, "Why not? What is there about feminism you don't like?"

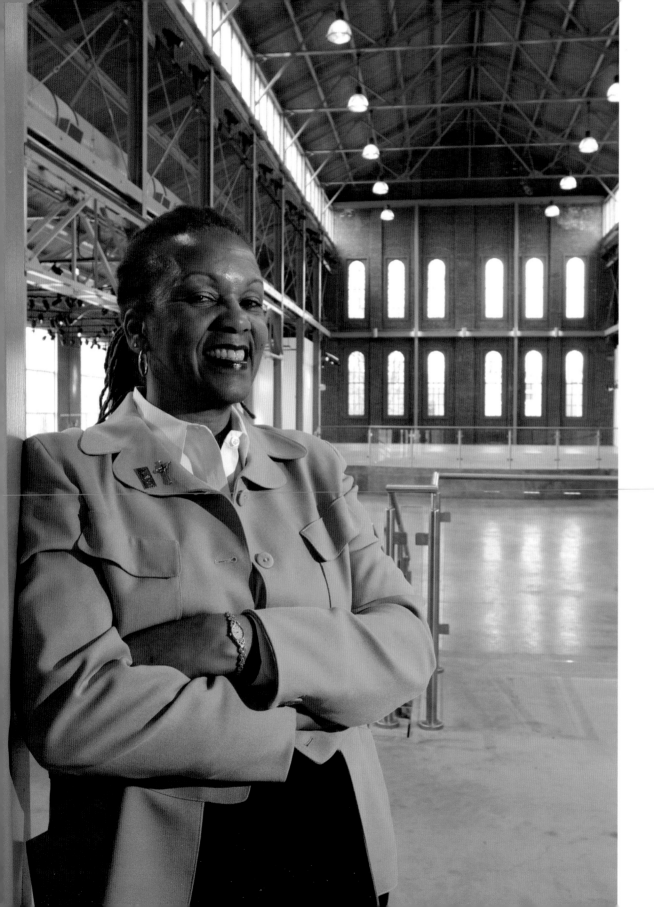

Rita Phillips

There's no hiding your enthusiasm for the future of the Kentucky Center for African American Heritage, an ambitious project of which you are the executive director.

The project has been on the table for many years. Our vision is to have it be a major tourism destination, but our mission is to educate the public regarding the remarkable history and culture of the African American people. We will have programs for youth, many exhibits, a genealogical research component, and a rental space. We've received huge corporate support and the help of wonderful volunteers. It has been a struggle to get this far, but we've been very fortunate in putting the pieces together so it will come to fruition and impact the community. It is the connector it was supposed to be.

You're very honest about your feelings and own experiences with racism.

I have experienced racism in the community and the workplace, but I haven't let that be a stumbling block. People often have misunderstandings about cultures other than their own. That's an important reason we're trying to raise awareness of African American culture. When people are engaged into the fabric of another community it helps them understand and respect differences.

The day after the infamous Rodney King incident, police officers arrested me outside my office, telling me I had earlier been speeding, which was not true. The arrest was an offshoot of the feelings and emotions generated around the Rodney King incident. It was pure harassment and completely unjustified. I had contacts and resources to help me deal with the situation, and I eventually filed a complaint. For someone who didn't have the advantage of those resources and contacts, the situation could have been very different.

Heading up a major not-for-profit organization is new to you. You career has veered in a couple of directions, but you say you've learned something valuable at each turn.

I have a master's degree in Urban Studies. When I first went to college I wanted to be a physical therapist, but found out I didn't have the right type of constitution. My emotions got in the way. I switched to health education and later set up school programs focused on preventive dentistry. But I had an entrepreneurial spirit and thought self-employment was the way to go. My husband and I started the first African American-owned and -operated travel agency in Kentucky. I also branched out into other areas and discovered that if people know and trust you, they're willing to come to the table and work with you in various ways.

What have been the most defining moments of your life?

At 12 years old, I developed a relationship with Christ. I remember the moment I met him, at a revival. It defined my life forever and has helped me make many choices. It has helped me stay on task, not that I haven't fallen, and I don't get off course, because we all do. The other defining moment was that of giving birth.

It's not uncommon to hear someone talk about how dramatically he or she has changed over the years. But that's not the way you look at your life.

There have been different seasons in my life, but the core person I was at 21 is the person I am today. I'm at a higher level of maturity, but I've always been in touch with who I am as a person and what my goals are. I probably have the reputation of being feisty, not a conformist. I've never felt uncomfortable speaking my mind.

A big part of who I am was determined by being raised by my grandmother. I think I was grown up before my time. I'm very connected with the real world without being tied up in stereotypes. I love people and believe we are all put here to be joyful; I try to not let anyone steal my joy. There are certain folks in life who are intent on wreaking havoc and spreading negativity, but I believe there's a positive spirit in the world.

Is there something you'd like to do that you haven't done?

I believe I am blessed as a person to bless others. I want to travel, especially to Africa, not just to have a holiday, but to impact the lives of others. If we don't get outside our boundaries of comfort and engage in new experiences, we're missing out on life. When I'm at the door facing death, I don't want any regrets that I didn't do certain things.

Rachel Platt

You're a television icon in Louisville. Why did you choose broadcasting as a career?

A college speech professor asked me if I had ever thought about broadcasting. He intervened and set me on my life path. Television just suited me and it clicked. I will always be grateful to him and will always appreciate teachers.

How does it feel to have such a well known face in town?

There's no running in and out of a store. Some people come to me to say hello and others give me story ideas. You'd be surprised at the great tips I've received in Kroger.

There are undoubtedly many stories that have had an impact on you. What are some of the most memorable ones you have covered?

The most memorable ones aren't about famous people; they're about everyday people who have been dealt a tragedy and have done something with their experience to affect other people's lives. There is one story I covered that will stay with me forever. I went to Vietnam with a group of men from Bardstown who wanted to go back to honor their fallen comrades. To be part of that and to cover it was a true privilege.

Is there a gender gap in broadcasting?

I'm at the age that it can be tougher for women. Most women get out of the business at about my age. I think sometimes broadcasting is more unforgiving for women than for men. Men can get gray hair and it's wonderful, but you don't see many women on television with gray hair, or their natural faces. It's still one of those bastions we need to overcome. As in many professions, women always feel like we have to be twice as good and work harder than anyone. Most of my contemporaries who are women are much like I am. We have earned our stripes without a doubt.

Did you ever make a faux pas on the air?

Oh, yes! One day I was discussing the Olympics with my colleague Ken Schulz. I commented that a skater had performed a triple lutz. After he made a smart aleck comment, I said, "You're such a putz." I said it because it rhymed with lutz. He later told me he couldn't believe I had said that on the air because it means a part of the male anatomy.

Your life recently changed in a big way.

Did it ever! I'm no longer doing the early morning show. I have to admit that the early schedule was great because I finished my shows early enough that I never missed any events in my kids' lives. But now I get to sleep a full eight hours at night and don't have to get up at 2 a.m. But I felt like a vampire coming to the station on my new schedule. I almost had to avert my eyes from the sun. And I had to get used to traffic. There hadn't been any at 3 o'clock in the morning.

What has been your most formidable challenge in your personal life?

Losing my father. When he was ill, I held on to his dog tags all the time. They're now on the frame of his picture that sits on my dresser. I talk to him often.

Do you have any major disappointments?

Only that I didn't get more sleep in this life.

What do you consider your most significant accomplishment?

It's still a work in progress! My children.

And the most defining moment in your life?

Becoming a mother. That changes everything. You're so out of yourself at that point. The "me" goes away because you're a mom first. It was life-altering in the best possible way.

What's the biggest risk you have ever taken?

The biggest physical risk was following a National Guard unit to Sarajevo during a cease fire. It was an amazing story to cover. We wore flak jackets the entire time. I thought I was going to be the wimp of our group, but the photographer and producer both came to my room because they were scared.

Other than the people in your life, what couldn't you live without?

Iced tea.

Do you have a secret indulgence?

Yes, it's a tacky one, the *National Enquirer*. But I don't go as low as the *Globe*. I'm highbrow.

Suzy Post

You have been a longtime advocate for civil and human rights. What do you believe have been your most significant accomplishments?
Desegregating the Jefferson County schools, implementing Title IX in the schools, and making it appropriate for a woman to stand up to authority, and win!

Do you think the protests and dramatic commitments to social causes that were prevalent in the past seem to have lost momentum?
No. I think a lot of that momentum is exactly what has fueled the LGBT movement so successfully.

What do you consider today's most important political and social causes?
Leveling the economic playing field to assure that every American household has enough to pay for enough food and adequate housing for its families. A living wage is where we have to start.

Because of the strong positions you have taken on various issues, you must have made some enemies. What do you have to say to them?
Not much. I am working for all of us to construct a livable society for all.

You have a great sense of humor . That must have served you well.
I guess it has kept me from feeling that anything I do is going to make much of a difference so I might as well not take myself too seriously.

What has been the biggest challenge in your life?
Holding on to a modicum of sanity for the eight years I was the ACLU Kentucky director.

What, if anything, do you regret?
Not keeping a journal. What a life!

Other than the people in your life, what couldn't you live without?
Chocolate.

What's the biggest risk you've ever taken?
Marrying. We were both very young when we married. That was the custom back then. Our brains had not developed.

Was it worth the risk?
Yes, it was worth it because I have five great kids.

What's the most important thing you've learned about yourself?
That I am very sloppy.

Is there anything that intimidates you?
No.

What has been the most defining moment in your life?
Winning the 34th legislative district in Gene McCarthy's bid for the presidency as the peace candidate. We beat the Party regulars.

What haven't you done that you would like to do?
Travel in the Far East.

What would people be surprised to know about you?
I adore my children. I think I come across as very tough and not very sensitive. That's not true. If anything, I'm very sensitive. You can't be involved in social justice unless you're very sensitive to the inequities in the world.

Is there anything you would change about yourself if you could?
I talk too much.

If you could be anywhere in the world right now, where would you be and what would you be doing?
In Florence having pasta and fried eggplant.

Finish the sentence, "I wish women would…..
be much more assertive."

If you could have dinner with anyone in the world, who would it be and why?
I'm a perfectly normal woman. If he hadn't died, Paul Newman. Why? You must be kidding. He was a perfect blending of sex appeal and good values.

What makes you happiest?
Being with my scattered-all-over-the-country five kids and their kids. I adore my adult children. They have a great sense of humor and good values. If I hadn't raised them I would talk about them all the time.

Gwynne Tuell Potts

You recently stepped down as president of Historic Locust Grove. Locust Grove was a gathering place for historical figures. The conversations sometimes must have represented divergent political philosophies. You aren't shy about sharing your political beliefs.

I'm a Democrat. Being a Democrat is important to me because I think it's an indicator of an interest in social justice. My husband, a Republican, thinks that the circus my party creates is entertaining, but he doesn't want to be part of it. Our conversations are respectful, but they can be heated. I imagine conversations at Locust Grove were much the same. George Rogers Clark considered himself to be a Citizen Republican in the French sense. In fact, at one point he became a French citizen and general, disavowing a connection to the United States. The distance of 230 years or so tends to dilute the passion involved in the creation of this nation, but those conversations were every bit as electric as today's political spars.

What was your experience of teaching in the public schools during a time of great turmoil in Louisville?

I was a young history teacher at Western High School when busing began in 1975, and unprepared, as everyone in the system was, for the situation in which I found myself and for the neighborhood's reaction. The parents weren't so much opposed to West End children coming to their neighborhood schools as they were afraid for their children to be sent to places they perceived to be dangerous. The faculty won most parents back the following year when the Jefferson County Teachers Association members went on strike. The neighborhood consisted of working people, and they understood strikes. They were great; they brought us food and hot coffee. Busing led to all kinds of internal and external evaluation of our public schools, and as a result, I believe the system emerged from the initial turmoil a far superior one to the pre-1975 district.

Do you consider yourself a strong woman?

I can be strong if I need to be. I think strong women like strong women. But it's the exceptional man who likes a strong woman.

What do you like best about yourself?

I'm usually optimistic. I seldom come up against something that can't be improved with enough work and attention. I have resources of energy for projects that capture my attention. I appreciate the idea that I'm not lazy. Thanks to all who helped me understand the world, I'm able to value order, beauty, talent, and goodness, and those things bring me great happiness. Also, I'm good to my dogs.

And least?

I'm a reactionary. I don't often say things I regret, but frequently say things in a way that I regret. I don't have patience for sloppy work or rudeness. I like people who are engaged, focused, and who contribute. I can be sharp with people for whom I have little respect.

What traits do you most admire in other people?

Intelligence, honesty, kindness, and humor, probably in that order. I can't say I'm opposed to contrarians, either, because they keep the debate sharp.

Do you think you've "found" yourself?

Not entirely, but I'm getting closer. I hope I will continue to grow. Maturity isn't all bad.

What are your major regrets?

The ability to find and embrace an intelligent spirituality has eluded me and, sadly, Presbyterianism seems increasingly meaningless. Also, I was unprepared for parenthood. It should be biologically impossible to reproduce before the age of 30. Thank goodness for grandchildren. They are life's mulligans.

Other than the people in your life, what couldn't you live without?

Books and dogs.

What would people be surprised to know about you?

That I'm extremely uncomfortable as a focus of attention.

Do you have any secret indulgences?

Chocolate and baseball, but many people would say that isn't a secret!

Is there anything you would change about yourself if you could?

I've never been able to chill with the girls; men's conversation usually seems more interesting and purposeful. I would like to be a better friend to women.

If you could be anywhere in the world right now, where would you be and what would you be doing?

Somewhere in northern Europe, in a library, understanding the dots that connect Western civilization.

Sharon Receveur

You have battled cancer twice, have suffered three heart attacks, had open heart surgery, and have heart failure. Do you ever wonder, "Why me?"

It has never occurred to me to ask that question. I have had a great run if it were all to end this minute. I am the luckiest chick to ever walk the face of the earth because of the people I have met and the things I have been able to do. My life is so full.

What has kept you going through the most difficult times with your health?

My gratitude. It's the basis of my spirituality.

Have you questioned God during your illnesses?

Sure. You clean out your closet, clean your desk, make sure your will is updated, and try to figure out the God thing. But it isn't so easy to figure it out. I don't think I'm supposed to. Every day is a new opportunity to have a conversation with God and to be in awe of something greater than myself. I think I will eventually ask God some questions, but he is going to ask one of me, "Have you looked for me—in my flowers, my people, my birds, my mountains?" I haven't done it all the time, but I try. I need to be prepared to answer that question.

You must want to kick people who complain about petty things.

Just because what they're complaining about may seem petty to me, it may be huge to them. What ticks me off more than anything is unfairness, such as a mother who has a sick child and no health insurance. In response to unfairness, I often write a letter but forbid myself to send it. The next morning I read it again, and if it is written out of anger and doesn't offer a solution to the problem as I see it, I still won't send it. I have to act out of wanting to correct a situation, not just bitch about it.

Do you believe in an afterlife?

I hope there is an afterlife because there are people who have lived before me who I really want to meet—the good, the bad, and the ugly. I especially want to meet Mother Teresa and Stalin. I'd ask him what he possibly could have been thinking. The same goes for Mao, who never brushed his teeth. I also want to meet Eleanor and Franklin Roosevelt, who had such an odd relationship and yet were so forward thinking. And, of course, I hope to meet my mom and dad and sister, people I have loved and lost.

My concept of heaven is not a bunch of angels playing harps and singing. It's more about being able to do all the things I have always wanted to do but was chicken to do for fear of killing myself.

You are very open about being a recovering alcoholic.

Getting and staying sober has been the most significant accomplishment of my life. Heart disease and cancer are awful, but alcoholism is so deadly, and kills not only you, but also your relationships. The times I would love to have a drink are few and far between. But when I was in so much pain with chemo, I wanted to chill out and mistakenly thought a drink would be therapeutic. I knew deep down it would do no such thing and never succumbed. In my 12 Step program we have a saying that one drink is too many and a thousand are not enough. I am powerless after the first one.

You're known for being an absolutely wonderful friend.

That's the highest compliment anyone could pay me. My friends have brought humor, honesty, and intelligence into my life.

What's the most important thing you've learned about yourself?

That I'm more capable than I thought of feeling and doing things that are hard.

Would it be trite to say that you live for today?

Perhaps it's a matter of semantics, but I think I live in today. If you have one foot in yesterday and one foot in tomorrow, you lose focus on today.

What would people be surprised to know about you?

Nothing. What you see is what you get. I have talked a lot about personal issues. What else is there? I have always thought that the best thing I could ever do is to tell my story because it's mine. No one can argue with it, and it might help someone. Well, there is one thing that might surprise people. I'm jealous of my husband's ability to cook.

After going through so much, is there anything that intimidates you?

Big machines.

Susan Reigler

You're a zoologist, biologist, and musician. You were also a science and travel writer for *The Courier-Journal* and you were the newspaper's food critic. Also, you're the author of several books about bourbon and a guide to Kentucky State Parks. Do you consider yourself a Renaissance woman?
I've been accused of that. I just have a lot of interests, which I suppose is unusual in a time of specialization.

Reading about and, sometimes, talking to you can be a little intimidating. You are very accomplished in several areas. Most people must seem very dull to you.
Not at all. Everyone has something they're passionate about and for which they have talents. Discovering that was always my job as a reporter. In teaching I always have great fun learning from my students' perspectives.

Your career as a food writer and food critic for *The Courier-Journal* was predestined, don't you think?
No, but an amusing coincidence happened the week I found out I got the job as food critic. I had dinner at a Chinese restaurant and when I opened my fortune cookie it read, "You can have your cake and eat it too." I had written several audition columns and even though one extolled the virtues of White Castle, they still hired me.

But that wasn't the beginning of your love of food.
No. I grew up eating a lot of traditional, wonderful cooking. My mother and grandmother were excellent Southern cooks. I appreciated quality rather than eating something out of a can. I was exposed to many different types of food and beverages while I lived in England. There I joined a wine club and learned that I could buy French wine for very little money. It was fascinating and fun. I loved English pub grub but also enjoyed Continental cuisine. When I got back to the United States, I figured I'd have to learn to cook if I was to eat the way I liked. I bought Julia Child's *Mastering the Art of French Cooking*. Anyone with patience and a keen eye can do it.

How did your life of music begin?
I was a musician from the time I was 10 years old, when I started playing trumpet in the school band. I also played the viola for about 20 years. I have had wonderful opportunities such as playing in several ensembles while at Oxford University. I was a founding member, and am a brass player, program annotator, and archivist for Ars Femina, an ensemble that plays on period instruments the work of female composers from 1500-1900. In my midlife crisis

I decided to get a music degree rather than buy a sports car. When I graduated, Indiana University Southeast needed someone to teach music appreciation. I had no intention of doing that, but now I sometimes teach in the music department as well as the biology department and I play in the university's orchestra and brass band, as well as in the Athena Brass Band, an all-women ensemble of players recruited from around the country.

Biology, zoology…it's interesting that you didn't confine yourself to one area of science.
Entomology is my specialty. The world is an intricate place. It's overwhelming. But the fun of being a scientist is seeing the patterns and understanding the wonder and connectedness. The complexity is beautiful.

As a zoologist, you have an interesting perspective on animals and humans. People think of animals in the context of us. We've been on the planet for a fraction of the time the planet has been here so our view is a little odd. We may be the only ones who can communicate our eccentricities in an effective way.

You're the resident consulting biologist at Blackacre State Nature Preserve. What does that involve?
It's a volunteer position, unless a grant has been received to support my work. For many years I've kept checklists of plant and animal species and worked with many school groups. My university research students and I also conducted an insect survey to determine if habitat restoration was working and if there has been a change in the insect population. Other faculty and students have conducted other kinds of surveys about plants and animals.
This is important information for habitat management and is used by the Kentucky State Nature Preserves Commission. All of that research is posted online so any scientist or member of the public can access it as well.

What haven't you done that you'd like to do?
Go to the Galapagos Islands. I'm torn about that because they have fragile ecosystems. Tourism is a mixed benefit/cost. I'd love to follow Darwin's footsteps, but I probably won't.

Babs Rodes
Robinson

You're continuing your family's legacy of philanthropy and of being actively involved in many organizations throughout Louisville. What are some of the causes with which you have a special connection?

I'm very proud of my family's history with some charities in Louisville. I grew up watching my family serve with these various groups, and as a result, I will always have a personal connection to these organizations. However, I will always hold a special place in my heart for Louisville Collegiate School as my sister and mother attended the school as well. As an alumnus, I truly value the school's academic mission and incredible educational value. As a parent, I have witnessed firsthand the school's positive effect on my children. As a board member, I enjoy working with the board to ensure the school's prosperous future for other generations. I also serve on the Cave Hill Cemetery board of directors. My father not only loved Cave Hill Cemetery, but he also valued its historical significance to Louisville. I love supporting my father's passion, and in the process, helping maintain a centerpiece for Louisville history. Although I just recently joined the James Graham Brown Cancer Center board, I have been aware of the Center for a long time as my father and uncle helped in its creation. The Cancer Center is a vital institution in the fight against cancer, and it's great to follow my family's dedication to the tremendous cause. I, along with my grandmother, both served on the Speed Art Museum board. My Grandmother imparted to me the importance for the arts. I enjoyed working on the Speed board, because the museum is pivotal in preserving and promoting the arts for our city.

It is understandable that as Louisville grows, its character may be changing. How do you view those changes?

In this day and age, change is constant. Louisville has dramatically changed over my lifetime, and all for the positive. However, even as the city changed in structure, it stays similar in culture. Louisville remains the same city, full of Southern charm and Midwestern hospitality in 2013 as it was when I was born here. Louisville is still the "big little city" full of immense local pride. Therefore, people continue to work and volunteer to make our city a perpetually better place. The causes might change year to year, but the charitable spirit in Louisville is ever-present.

What motivates and inspires you?

As a parent, I believe that you should always try and make a place better than you found it. I'm motivated by the belief that I want my children and the next generation to enjoy the very organizations and institutions that I enjoyed as a child. It is inspirational to witness and work with so many people who selflessly volunteer to improve their surroundings in the local community.

What has been the biggest challenge in your life?

It was very difficult for me when my older sister passed away, as Mary had such an energetic personality and was dedicated to our family. She was the glue that kept my family together, so when she passed away, I found myself with many new responsibilities I was not yet prepared for.

Other than the people in your life, what couldn't you live without?

Dark chocolate. It's my guilty pleasure.

What's the biggest risk you've ever taken?

Having an outdoor wedding during the year of the cicadas, 26 years ago.

What's the most important thing you've learned about yourself?

That the simplest answer is usually the best answer. Being straightforward is key.

Is there anything that intimidates you?

No, not much.

What has been the most defining moment in your life?

I like to think I have three defining moments: our sons.

What haven't you done that you would like to do?

Travel to the summer Olympics.

Is there anything people would be surprised to know about you?

I'm not nearly as tough as people think. I always laughed when my kids would tell me that their friends were afraid of me.

What's the best decision you have ever made?

Marrying Lee.

What do you like best about yourself?

I believe in my strong work ethic.

And least?

I have trouble saying no.

If you could be anywhere in the world right now, where would you be and what would you be doing?

In Monte Carlo, relaxing on the beach.

Vicki Rogers

You majored in telecommunications to prepare for your broadcast career. But you also had a secret ambition.

I was in a rock band, Visions, in high school. I thought I would be a rock star, but I knew I had to have a backup plan. I now sing with a few bands around town.

Before you became a Lite 106.9 radio personality, you were a behind-the-scenes media person.

After graduating with a telecommunications degree, I first got a job as a media buyer. It paid very little and wasn't at all what I wanted, but it got my foot in the door of the radio and television world. I started doing voice-overs for radio and television commercials and did some comedy bits on *The Bob & Tom Show* in Indianapolis. When I moved to Louisville, I was hired in sales at 106.9, and did some voice-overs for the station. Then I got the on-air job. I love it. I like trying to make someone's day a little better by what I talk about on the show.

Isn't it hard to be so cheery and happy on the radio every day?

I'm an optimistic person. People say I always sound happy on the radio. Ninety-eight percent of the time I am happy. The other two percent of the time I'm a good actress.

Your show is casual and upbeat, but that changed the morning of 9/11.

I was on the air when the second plane hit the World Trade Center. We went to news feeds and I would talk and take phone calls periodically so that people could express their feelings. For the next several days we cried with people, read letters, and shared stories. It was a very moving, emotional experience.

How do you respond when someone says that "radio isn't what it used to be"?

I don't think local radio will ever go away. People want to listen to people who know them, and those of us in local radio want to talk to them.

What's it like to be driving in a car listening to the radio or sitting on the sofa watching television and suddenly hear your voice on a commercial?

It's fun. It makes my kids proud, and they think it's kind of cool. But I'm very critical. I listen and think about how I should have said things differently.

Are you able to let your hair down when you go out? Or are you always concerned about how you look, what you do, and what you say?

It's kind of hard sometimes. I have to behave myself. Sometimes I would like to go out without makeup, but I usually don't. It's nice to go on vacation, to get away and not have to worry about it.

You're very active in community and charitable events. What organizations are especially important to you?

I've been involved with the March of Dimes as well as the Leukemia and Lymphoma Society for quite awhile. The Alzheimer's Association has asked me to work with them, and I'd like to do that. We broadcast every year from the St. Joe's Picnic. It's a wonderful cause and one in which I take a personal interest.

A new chapter in your life had an unexpected start.

I went on a blind date not expecting much. It was almost love at first sight. We got married and are living happily ever after. He is such a kind and generous man and is my soul mate. With him, my children, my parents, and brother, my life is complete.

How do you like to spend your spare time?

I didn't take it up until I was 35 years old, but I'm a pretty decent tennis player. I'm on several women's teams and also play mixed doubles. That I was a high school athlete—track and gymnastics—probably helps. I also like to play the guitar, drums, piano, and harmonica.

Is there anything you'd like to change about yourself?

I'm a little afraid to stand up for myself. But I'm getting tougher as I get older.

What, other than the people in your live, couldn't you live without?

My guitar. I love my guitar.

Does anything intimidate you?

Not really. I'm rather bold and self-confident.

What's the biggest risk you've taken?

I'm not a risk taker. I'm a big chicken.

What haven't you done that you'd like to do?

I want to do a voice over for a Disney film.

Rabbi
Gaylia R. Rooks

Your journey to becoming Senior Rabbi at The Temple – Congregation Adath Israel Brith Sholom was remarkable and full of a great deal of pain.
I knew I wanted to be a rabbi when I was in the 10th grade even though, at that time, there were no female rabbis. My father disowned me when I went to rabbinical school. He wanted me to go to law school. "I have never met a rabbi I didn't hate," he said. I had to question whether becoming a rabbi was worth giving up my relationship with him. Although he came to my wedding, he didn't speak to me. We were estranged for many years. I learned about unconditional love from my husband and his family. That gave me the strength to call my father every year on the various holidays.

You achieved a couple important "firsts."
I was one of the first women to attend the Hebrew Union College, and was the only woman my year to attend its Los Angeles campus. My classmates were very supportive but there were a few professors who didn't believe in ordaining women. Also, I was the first female rabbi in Kentucky. Louisville is very Southern. Some people may have had difficulty with the concept of a woman rabbi, but ultimately most of them found the reality was not as threatening as they thought.

Same-sex marriage is one of today's most emotional issues. You have performed same-sex marriages. What do you say to people who oppose the unions?
God created each of us with our own special gifts and it seems to me to take quite a lot of chutzpah to challenge the infinite wisdom of our Creator. I have always been proud to be part of Reform Judaism, a movement that has long stood in the forefront of just and righteous causes.

Do you ever question God or your faith?
Living in a post-Holocaust world I think it's hard not to question. I like to use the image of a tapestry and think of God as the Weaver. As humans, we're able to see only the back of the tapestry—the knots, fragments, and ends. Only God can understand the overall design and sacred pattern on the front.

It can be heartbreaking to watch a person struggling with how they believe God may be part of their lives. When I was a chaplain at Jewish Hospital, one of the hardest things I have ever done was to talk with a man whose wife was dying of cancer. He believed he was being punished for not being a good husband and father. While the role of interfaith chaplain is to meet people where they are in their own faith, it was very hard for me not to try and convince him that he was not being punished. A God who would take the life of a young woman to force her husband to be a better person is just not part of my theology.

Do you believe in miracles?
I believe in miracles because I believe in love. But I don't believe God usually chooses to work through miracles because that "interferes" with our free will. Rather, God created this world with laws of nature that are at work. When a tree gets hit by lightning and falls, it doesn't matter how righteous the person standing underneath has been. Also, I don't believe that prayer is like some cosmic candy machine that you push the right buttons and out pops your request. Prayer has great power but not as merely some form of currency with God.

Why do you bristle when people talk about tolerance?
I never use the word "tolerance." I much prefer "respect." I don't want to be tolerated. I want to be respected and entitled to my own beliefs. I think everyone deserves this but many people are so convinced that only their way is the right way.

Other than the people in your life, what couldn't you live without?
Music has always been my best path to God. When my son was first diagnosed with autism I damaged my vocal chords from crying so much. It ended up that I couldn't sing at a time when I needed God the most. My most spiritual and familiar pathways to God were inaccessible and that made everything much harder. Fortunately, even in that dark place, God was there. My son has grown into an amazing young man, my voice returned as did my sense of God's Presence in our lives. The music was never really gone... I just needed some time to hear it again.

Debbie
Scoppechio

You founded Creative Alliance advertising agency 25 years ago. What do you consider your greatest triumphs?
Winning the KFC national print contract and the Kentucky Lottery contract catapulted us to become the largest agency in Kentucky.

You've worked with some of the most well-known companies in the country. What client have you not worked with that you'd like to have as a client?
Any pet-related company, whether pet food or pet toys. We're pet-centered at the agency, and I love animals.

What has made you, personally, so successful?
My passion for the business, and not being afraid to take risks and to work hard. Also, I get personally involved with our clients and their businesses.

What makes you a good leader?
Having great followers. Sharing my expectations, goals, and objectives. Leading by example. Developing a recognition culture. But keeping everyone motivated all the time is hard. I have a work hard/play hard attitude for all of us, and I do both.

Would you want to work for you?
There are a number of reasons I would and a couple of reasons I wouldn't. I'm demanding and have high expectations. We have about 15 people who have left and have come back. Hopefully, they all love working for me, but not because I'm easy. I care greatly about each one of them.

You're Chief Executive Officer and your husband is Chief Operating Officer of your company. Isn't that a lot of closeness at the office?
If someone had told me they were going to do that, I wouldn't have recommended it. But our roles are very different and we don't really see each other every day at work. We have had exactly one argument at work in 23 years. Frankly, I don't know that any other man would live with me because of the hours I work and spend with clients. So, from that aspect, working together is a positive.

You were diagnosed with breast cancer, then a brain tumor. How did those experiences change you?
The breast cancer was six years ago. Having it made me appreciate my teammates, friends, and family even more. I learned to live every day as if it's my last. I concentrate on enjoying today because you don't know what's going to happen tomorrow. A year ago I tripped over my Pekingese and hit my head.

A CT scan found a nonmalignant brain tumor. But brain surgery revealed a breast cancer-related tumor under it. The good news was they found it, but the bad news was there was still cancer in my body. I had radiation. It was then I started to really think about what I'm going to do the rest of my life. The follow-ups have been great and I'm doing very well.

What are the biggest risks you have ever taken?
In my personal life, probably getting a divorce from my first husband, and moving to Louisville. But I'm still best friends with him, and moving to Louisville was the best thing I ever did.

What's the most important thing you've learned about yourself?
Sometimes it's caring too much about people and their families. I have learned that can be harmful in business.

Is there anything that intimidates you?
Absolutely not.

What has been your major disappointment?
I can't think of any major ones.

Other than the people in your life, what couldn't you live without?
Chocolate and animals.

What do you like best about yourself?
My sense of humor and passion for living.

And least?
My occasional bad moods.

What would people be surprised to know about you?
People think I'm a businesswoman who's driven and will do anything to get ahead. That's really not me. I care about people much more than outsiders think. On a personal level, people would be surprised to know that I danced on the Ed Sullivan Show when I was 13 years old.

Finish the sentence, "I wish women would…
not worry about being a woman versus a man". It's all about being a person. And never being intimidated about anything.

Is there anything you would change about yourself if you could?
I'd eat better, exercise more and take better care of my health. On the other hand, I've been through two bouts of cancer and I pretty much want to do what I want to do.

Barbara Sexton Smith

When you were asked to assume the position of President and CEO of the Fund for the Arts following a difficult time in the organization's history, did you ever consider declining?

No. I felt it was the right thing to do for the community. It wasn't really up to me to choose. It was a calling and I didn't question the calling. I'm a student and practitioner of the Servant Leader Model, meaning that I understand that none of it is about me. I'm simply the vehicle through which the mission is accomplished. The job itself is a vehicle in which I have been placed to travel this journey on a much greater mission to leave the earth better than we found it. Some people would say I never say no. But I believe we're a long time dead so we need to get busy while we're here.

How important is faith in your life?

I'm extremely grounded in my faith. It's who I am, what I am, and why I am. You don't know God is all you need until God is all you've got. I learned that staring down the barrel of a sawed-off shotgun while I was crouched on the floor at a Wendy's restaurant where I was in all my glory working as an assistant manager. It changed my life forever.

You wrote *Speaking of Success* in which successful people told their stories. What motivates and inspires you to be successful?

If you were in a foxhole, you'd want me next to you. I'm very centered and grounded and determined to take people to a place they never thought they could reach. Whenever I'm facing a crisis I like to create a different rhythm. It all goes back to when I was growing up. In our house one could never say, "I can't."

Do you think women and men view success differently?

Men evaluate their level of success based on their independence. For them, there's only one king of the hill and you have to knock people down to get ahead. Women evaluate levels of success based on our relationships. We want to take people with us along the way.

You're very driven. Are you a Type A personality?

I'm sure I am.

You seem to be constantly in motion—physically and mentally. Don't you wear even yourself out?

I exhaust myself on a daily basis. And I believe I'm completely exhausting. Is that a good thing? I'm not sure.

What is the most important lesson you have learned?

I have grown more in the past two years than in my first 30 years in business. I have learned how incredibly difficult it is to understand people's perceptions and manage them when they couldn't be farther from reality, and how difficult it is to remain patient and calm while others are taking what seems to be an eternal amount of time to grasp the concept.

People tend to love me or hate me. It used to hurt my feelings and break my heart, but that's okay. Everyone doesn't have to like me.

You have a different take on PMS.

Hope is my favorite word and emotion. It's my touchstone. I think it's important that you have PMS—a personal mission statement. Mine is to instill hope in the hearts of everyone I meet. Hope is having only positive expectations.

What do you like best about yourself?

I find humor in most things. I look for the lighter side of things.

The fear of public speaking is very common. You spend a great deal of time in front of groups. Do you have any advice that would help conquer the fear?

My greatest fear was public speaking but I had to overcome the fear to pave the way for doors to open. Long before I knew I was afraid of public speaking, my father told me that if you're walking to a microphone and aren't nervous, don't go, because if you aren't nervous you're not ready to give your best.

What would people be surprised to know about you?

That my husband and I spend a lot of time memorizing poetry and go to great lengths to get every word right.

What's next for you?

Find a way for all of us to cross Ninth Street. It goes both ways. The West End needs to come east and the East End needs to come west.

Nancy Shepherd

You say that everyone "has a story," but you have to admit yours is unusually dramatic.

I married my high school sweetheart, when I was 20 years old. I thought I'd live happily ever after. We had a wonderful daughter almost immediately. He was, and is, the nicest man in the world, but I realized it wasn't a good marriage. He was happy having a job, house, wife, and child. He was settled. I didn't want to settle. I wanted more. I wanted to know what was out there. I got a divorce and kept teaching high school English, and began trying to figure out what I was going to do with my life.

Your second husband, architect and restaurateur David Shepherd, was a charismatic, brilliant man. Love at first sight turned into a tumultuous marriage.

When we first met, I never thought anything would come of it because he was such a wild thing. We married and fell in love with food and cooking. We became friends with people in Louisville's culinary world. In 1981, we opened Café Metro, which really introduced Louisville to the concept of fine dining. I continued to teach school during the day and worked "in the front of the house" at the restaurant at night. When you're teaching, you can't smoke and drink at work, so being at the restaurant was lots of fun. The restaurant was immediately successful. David became easily bored and wanted to open a second restaurant. I wanted to name it Harry Bailey because Harry Bailey was the inn master in *Canterbury Tales*. A friend told us the space was formerly named the Uptown Café. That became the restaurant's name. It, too, became very successful. Sadly, David had trouble handling our successes and the marriage failed.

Your first major health problem was nearly fatal.

I had a brain hemorrhage and was given a 25 percent chance of survival. I went through months of recovery and rehabilitation. I had to learn to read, write, and walk again. I didn't have any trouble with speech. As my mother was quick to point out, I never lost my mouth. I was painfully honest. Whatever I thought came out of my mouth. It still does.

Soon after, a fire in your house challenged your stamina and perseverance once again.

It could have been much worse. I never thought "Why me?" My parents would have expected me to pick up and continue. I had no choice other than that. I believe in angels. There's something out there that helps us when we need help.

Only months later, you had to deal with another tragedy.

I received a call that David had been killed in a car accident. I had always been the face of Café Metro but hadn't worked following the brain hemorrhage. I took over the operations of the two restaurants.

Having to close Café Metro must have been devastating to you.

It had been a Louisville icon for years. I realized the faltering economy and the demise of fine dining threatened the restaurant, but it took quite awhile before I admitted it was doomed. Closing was very difficult for me because my identity was so closely tied to the restaurant. I saw a counselor for a brief period. Things are better now. I have more time to read and to spend with my friends.

In a few words, how would you describe yourself?

Warm, bold, and sometimes brash.

When you look back on your life, what do you see?

I've done most everything I've wanted to do. I'm proud that I was a good teacher and took it very seriously. There's no job in the world more important than teaching. I feel pretty fulfilled in life. I regret that I was the world's greatest enabler. I also wish I had not spent entirely too much time with a troubled husband and not more time with my daughter.

You're very forthcoming about your feelings and experiences. Is there something that would surprise people to learn about you?

I'm not going to reveal it. I want to maintain the mystery.

What do you like best about yourself?

I'm genuine. I'm interested in and like people. I've found that if you're positive and kind, they'll generally respond the same way. What you give, you get back.

What trait do you most admire in others?

Integrity. I think it's lacking in many people because they sell themselves to please others. I may have sold myself at some point but, luckily, I don't recall it.

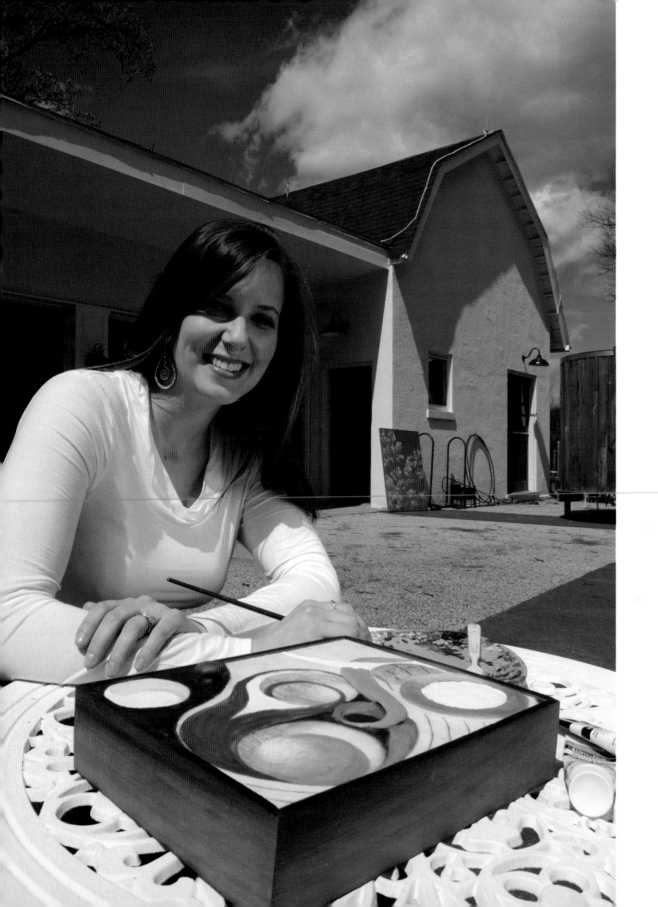

Maria Shore

You're an emerging artist. Did you ever consider another path in life?

I took photography and oil painting classes. Time flew by when I painted. I enjoyed it but didn't know how I would make a living doing it. I was on a biology/pre-med track for a year and a half. I chose a drawing and composition class as an elective, and immediately fell in love. When I finished my first drawing, I knew I could be an artist. That first piece is hanging in my family room now.

How did your parents react to the news that you were abandoning science for art?

Making the phone call to tell them wasn't easy. At first they were taken aback because the goal was for me to have a "real job." Surprisingly, they were both very supportive and said if that's what I wanted to do, to do it wholeheartedly.

Studying abroad gave you new perspectives.

I spent a summer in Scotland exploring photojournalism and a semester in Italy studying art history. It was hard to come back, and it's still hard to think I came back! The two experiences were so different, but each had a dramatic impact on me. Living in Milan was very challenging even though I grew up in an Italian American family and was quite familiar with the culture. I wasn't fluent in Italian but I tried very hard to fit in. It was wonderful, but I was terribly lonely at times.

What inspires your paintings?

That's a hard question. I don't feel like I get inspiration from the outside. Most of it comes from within. Colors inspire me the most. Most of my abstracts are very color-based.

Do you worry that you could be a starving artist?

Sometimes. I've had a couple of those years so far. Some months are lucrative and other months are tight, making me wonder if being a full-time artist is feasible. It can be hard to stay motivated and to keep going in the direction I want. I do some commercial work to help pay the bills. I'm hoping one day I'll look back and laugh about what I did in the early days.

What do you like best about yourself?

I'm very outgoing.

And least?

I'm not very decisive. I flip flop on my ideas. I'll start working on one piece, then five minutes later start on another one.

What would you do if you weren't an artist?

I don't know. I'd probably be on the street. I can't imagine not being an artist. As a volunteer for Hearts in Motion, I went to Guatemala. There were nurses and dentists in our group who held health clinics. I wasn't involved in the health aspect of the trip. Instead, I painted murals in a home for the elderly. It was very rewarding. So, if I weren't an artist, I might join the Peace Corps or Teach America.

Is there anything you'd change about yourself if you could?

I'd like to have more confidence in my work. It's something I never thought I'd have a problem with, but now that I'm doing larger pieces, it's become more of an issue.

What trait do you most like in a person?

Honesty. There's something so intriguing about people when you can tell they're not hiding anything.

And least?

Materialism. And I dislike when it surfaces in me. It's a battle for me to figure out what I really want and what I really need.

Who's the most fascinating person you know?

My mother. She is very ambitious and is continually growing. She's an attorney, has opened businesses, and is very well-rounded. Most of all, she's very kind. I think of a lot of people in business let that part go.

Melissa Sparks

You were involved in a tragic accident as a teenager. How has that impacted the person you are today?

When I was 18 years old, I was involved in a car accident that resulted in the death of my college roommate. This was a life-changing event and it's still never too far from my thoughts. For many years I had an immense amount of "survivor's guilt," wondering why I had lived and she didn't. I may never really know the answer to that question, but the moment I held my first daughter I began to understand maybe what God's purpose for my life was to be. The accident helped me realize early on how fragile life is, and to spend whatever time we have on Earth trying to make things better and enrich the lives of those around us.

There were more tests of your courage and strength.

I had a second car accident eight years later. I was knocked off the road and my car flipped over a 25-foot embankment before coming to rest upside down, but I escaped largely unscathed.

The one positive result of this accident is it led me to meet my future husband when I was in need of a rental car and a good friend connected me to Shawn to help me with my situation. We hit it off and have been married for 12 years.

When we wanted to start a family we ran into "unexplained infertility" that began years of failed treatments and several miscarriages. This was a devastating time for us, but it eventually led us to two of the greatest blessings of our lives—our internationally adopted daughters Leah and Kate.

While we were dealing with infertility as a couple, Shawn developed a chronic illness that causes him great difficulty breathing. Later, he was diagnosed with an aggressive form of cancer and spent several months undergoing very difficult and painful chemotherapy treatments. Thankfully, he has since recovered and the cancer has been in remission.

In spite of all of these difficulties, or maybe even because of them, we have grown stronger as a family and grown deeper in our faith. Looking back, what on one hand could be seen as the worst times of our lives have actually resulted in some of the most positive experiences of our lives. The accident helped bring my future husband and me together; our infertility helped lead us to adoption; our medical struggles helped us be open to a special-needs adoption; and Shawn's cancer helped us grow stronger spiritually.

Why did you choose foreign adoption?

Adoption has always been a part of my life. I was adopted at age four, so the idea that I would one day adopt had always been in the back of my mind. When I was a teenager, I saw an adorable Asian girl with an American family, and I told my mom that I would do the same. One day, at the exact moment Shawn and I were walking in Cherokee Park and discussing whether or not to adopt, and whether to do so internationally or domestically, a cherub-faced Asian toddler and her Caucasian father passed us and smiled the biggest, heartwarming grin. We knew right then and there that we most certainly would adopt, and our daughter would be from China.

After more than 18 months, we received a referral for a happy, healthy ten-month-old baby girl who we named Leah. She is the light of our lives, and we are crazy, head over heels in love with her.

We wanted to adopt another child from China. After years of dealing with Shawn's medical issues, we felt a strong calling to request a special-needs child. It took three years before we received a referral for a 21-month-old toddler girl who was born with only four functional fingers.

With only a couple of photos and limited medical information, we took a leap of faith. We are so glad we did because Kathryn Mei Lin (Chinese meaning "beautiful gem") is simply amazing. She knows no boundaries, and has a strong determination and fighting spirit that will carry her through all the challenges life will surely deliver.

What's the most important thing you've learned about yourself?

We have a plaque that says, We Can Do Hard Things. That's the most important thing I've learned about myself. Although life is full of difficulties and sometimes you just feel like throwing in the towel, don't give up. You may surprise yourself with how resilient you actually are.

What would people be surprised to know about you?

My free time during the years I spent on tennis courts led to a side hobby, juggling. It's lots of fun, and a great stress reliever!

Hollis Starks

You were catapulted into running a major business. Did you ever think of running away from the challenge?

Absolutely not. After I was divorced with a son, I went back to school for business courses and was determined to be a successful single mother. My mother had such a huge influence on me because she was a very successful career woman. I didn't have a positive feeling about staying home and taking care of a baby. When my father passed away, I inherited 50 percent of a company, a men's hat business that was outdated. We had second- and third-generation employees. I wanted to take on the challenge of keeping it going. I liked the garment and accessory business because I could figure it out; it was a natural for me. I also enjoyed the opportunity to re-create the business. I changed the customer base, making it a national business.

Eventually you had to make a very difficult business decision.

People in the industry had a lot of respect for me. I was the only woman running a large company of that type. But we had to close the business because of the economy. I was able to successfully deal with that because I had evolved enough as a female and a person to be able to separate emotion and sentimentality from the business model. My employees understood and stuck it out with me. It was a perfect balance of good people trying to do something the best possible way.

Now you're in the business of making people happy.

I recently created a special events business. I plan weddings and other significant events. The business enables me to get to know people on a level that means the world to me. I'm able to tap into a part of myself that's very sensitive to other people, their cultures and traditions. I love helping people make good memories.

But you also treasure the memories you create in your own home.

Our home is central to our family's life. I'm very artistic and think my canvas is to make my house beautiful. I love antiques and home accessories because they express who I am.

How did marrying into one of Louisville's oldest families of privilege impact your life?

I didn't really think about it when I got married, and still don't. I just thought I had married into a nice group of kind people. They're very low-key. Both of my parents and my brother are dead. I feel that my husband's family is my family, but don't think of myself as rich. I connected to my husband later in life. He had always had a soft spot in his heart for me. He's an artist and I thought he was the coolest thing. My marriage has been a wonderful vehicle for my evolution as a person. Our family expanded with the birth of our son. My husband is a very hands-on parent. We split up all the responsibilities of raising a family and that has been very important to both of us.

You're a world traveler. Do you have a bit of wanderlust?

I traveled extensively when I had the hat company. Now I frequently travel with a group of girlfriends. We "ran away from home" four years ago on a wonderful trip to France. We recently went to Turkey on another unbelievable trip. And my husband and I love to go to France. So, yes, although I enjoy being at home, sometimes I can't wait to get away to fabulous places.

There's a lot of juggling going on in your life.

I'm busy, and that's great. One of the most important parts of my life is fund-raising and being involved in causes that are dear to me. I'm especially proud of being on the board of the Morton Center, which supports the recovery of alcoholics and their families.

What do you like best about yourself?

I'm a generous friend with my time and emotions. My friends tell me that I inspire and motivate them. They know that I'm accessible and they feel safe with me.

And least?

I'm always on the move. I'd like to just "be" and not feel that I have to always "do."

What would people be surprised to know about you?

Although I'm very outgoing and friendly, there's part of me that's shy on the inside.

What are the traits you most like in a person?

Bravery, loyalty, compassion, and honesty.

And least?

Hypocrisy, selfishness, cruelty, and dishonesty.

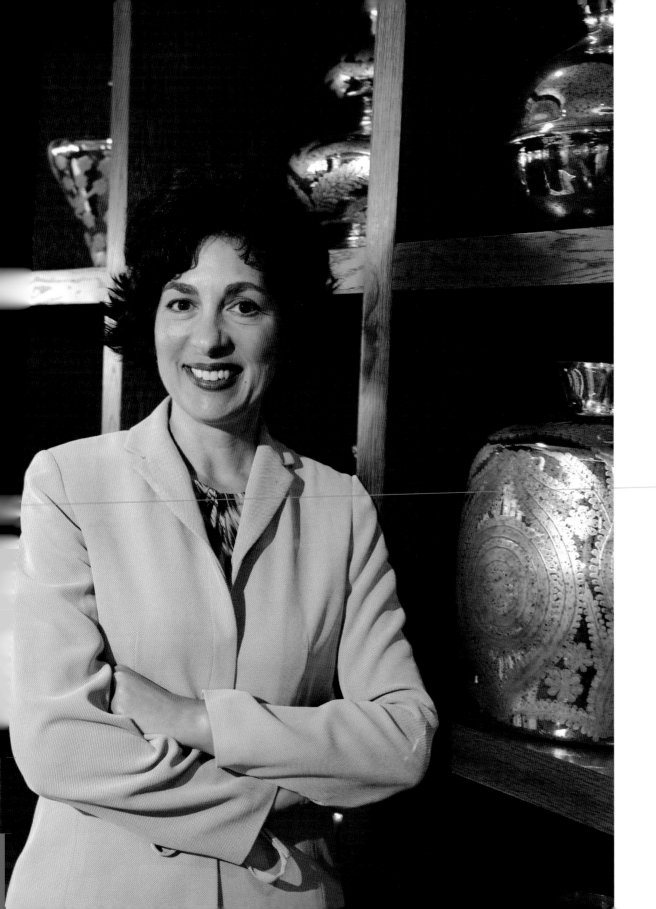

Peggy Noe
Stevens

You're the world's first female Master Bourbon Taster. That's an interesting "first."

When I worked at Brown-Forman I was involved in hospitality projects such as Woodford Reserve distillery and other brand destinations, such as those for Jack Daniels and Fetzer Wines. I recognized that I had a natural affinity for understanding product and complex flavor profiles. To become a Master Bourbon Taster I trained with the plant manager and worked closely with the master distiller. I didn't realize for quite some time that I was the first woman to achieve that title.

First you were a taster, and then you were a founder of Bourbon Women.

I used to conduct bourbon tastings across the country. The groups were predominantly male, although women would often approach me after a seminar. Many of them remember bourbon as what their fathers drank, but they wanted to be educated about it. I gathered some women I really respect, and we formed Bourbon Women. It's a great platform for starting a conversation about bourbon. It's also a wonderful platform for celebrating the heritage and lifestyle of Kentucky, and is a great networking opportunity.

An entrepreneurial spirit led you away from corporate life to start your own image branding and experiential marketing company. That sounds impressive, but what is it?

We focus on people and places. The people side encompasses image consultation, and training in etiquette, protocol, presentation, and nonverbal communications. The place side of the business involves working with brands and companies on messaging, Web sites, and marketing—an overall perspective of looking at their image.

You're the ultimate "people person." You have a new book that encourages others to be more people-oriented.

The Human Protocol of Business is all about getting back to some of the basics of being with people. In our digital age, we avoid conversations in lieu of communicating through e-mail and texting and Facebook, especially in business. Managers don't have that all-important connection to employees anymore. The book discusses how to put everything I teach in my business into practice.

Are you a person who has to be in control?

Yes, but the older I get, the better I delegate. It's a compliment when I delegate to someone because it shows that I give them my full trust. When I say to take the ball and run with it, I mean it.

What has been the most defining time of your life?

When my father died of cancer. He was my hero. He was such a gentleman and was the most unselfish man I've ever met. I regret that I didn't spend more time with him. My greatest disappointment has been that my sons didn't have longer to be around him and to learn from him. His death made me begin to look at life as being shorter and more precious. It was the catalyst that led to my starting my own company. It got me off the dime. I asked myself, "What am I waiting for?"

In a few words, how would you describe yourself?

Extroverted, energetic, optimistic. I'm always looking for the big picture.

What do you like best about yourself?

I don't let myself down. I'm a big fan of myself. I always pick myself up very quickly. I don't think a lot of people can do that.

So, do you think you have a big ego?

I'm a very confident woman, but no, I don't have a big ego. I still like to learn and I'm a very curious person.

Is there anything people would be surprised to know about you?

As social as I am, and as much entertaining as I do, I really like private time to be by myself to read and focus and write.

Soon you'll be an empty-nester. Are you ready for that?

I'm terrified. I'm very involved in my boys' lives. We have fun, we talk. I know everything that's going on with them. The transition is going to be difficult.

What, other than the people in your life, couldn't you live without?

Bourbon and all kinds of music. I have an eclectic palate for music. I also adore cooking and entertaining. And being with my friends and family. My son commented on how many girlfriends I have. Lucky me. They all bring different things to my life.

How do you feel about aging?

It doesn't bother me one bit. I'll never define myself by age.

Is there anything you would change about yourself if you could?

My impatience. It has probably tripped me up, but it also has made me successful.

Cherie Suchy

You were a sex therapist but say you suffered from burnout. What happened?

I've read that the average burnout time for a therapist is seven years. I lasted eight so I beat the average. It wears on you. I was a marriage and family therapist and had special training in sex therapy. That seemed a natural part of marriage and family counseling because sex plays a big part in most individuals' lives. There's definitely a need for it although I discovered that most people who could benefit from it don't seek it out. They shy away from it because they don't understand what help is available, they think it's embarrassing or they think someone will pass judgment on them. Even married people who had been together for a long time were bashful about saying to their partner what they wanted or liked or didn't like. Being direct about those things is very sexy and gets the ball rolling. There's about a 50/50 ratio of men and women who seek sex therapy. It's always most helpful when couples come together, but that doesn't always happen.

How did you transition from helping people with sex to helping horses with sex?

For awhile I was a writer for *The Thoroughbred Record* magazine and had opportunities to visit horse farms. That led to a job booking mares to the studs on former Kentucky governor Brereton Jones' farm. You could say I was a very high-priced madam. Not too many women were booking mares at that time. Some of the farm managers were hesitant to discuss with me cycles and ovulation and sperm life. I had to break some of the guys in. I got to meet such interesting people. Two of my clients were John Forsythe and Don Amici, both lovely men.

You joke that you now run a hen house. Please explain!

We went to garden shows and read a lot of magazines when we were landscaping our yard. We read about a man in the Highlands who was raising chickens. We decided to do it too. You might be surprised to know that urban chicken farming is a big thing, so much so that Jefferson County has a regulation that if you have less than half an acre you can have only five noncrowing fowl and one crowing fowl. We have four breeds of girls who lay fresh eggs. My husband built a Swiss chalet for them complete with shutters, window boxes, heating, and air conditioning. The chickens are named after family members they resemble. We get brown, green, pink, and blue eggs. It's awesome. Chickens are very low-maintenance, are quiet, don't stink, and are fun to watch. We sit on the patio drinking wine and watching the chickens. We're easily amused. One day they will stop laying eggs and we'll have a retirement home for hens.

When you're not collecting chicken eggs, you're selling houses.

I love selling real estate. Occasionally I'll have someone who's a pill to work with. But for the most part it's fun because clients are happy when you help them find a house.

You're also head of a charitable trust. What does it fund?

The Renau Foundation concentrates on three areas: humanitarian causes, animal welfare and writing. We've given a million dollars to Habitat for Humanity in Louisville, and we're building a house. Mr. Renau was a writer and wanted to provide writing scholarships. We award about $15,000 a year to high school seniors interested in writing. And we continue to support animal charities.

What haven't you done that you'd like to do?

I think I'd like to go back to school. I have an odd interest in geology. I'd also like to travel more. We've been to Paris and Prague and Barcelona. I always wanted to go to the South Pacific so my husband took me there for an anniversary. Now I have Istanbul on my mind. We also go to New York a lot because my daughter is a Rockette.

You seem to have a very positive, upbeat attitude.

I'm an eternal optimist. I think that you get what you look for in life. If you look for good things to happen and for things to go well, that's what you find. If you look for things to go wrong, they will.

What traits do you most like in a person?

Honesty, a sense of fun, and a sense of humor.

What don't you like in people?

Grumpiness, sneakiness, and dishonesty.

Rebecca Terry, M.D.

When did you decide to become a physician?
There was never any question. One of our family pictures shows me receiving a doctor's kit at Christmas when I was three years old. And, although I don't remember it, but according to my mother, I would tell my two sisters that they were very sick. I'd turn bubble bath into a poultice, hold them down, and wrap them up with it.

Your parents had an enormous influence on you.
My father was a minister in Cadiz, Kentucky. After he participated in the March on Washington with Martin Luther King Jr., incredibly, members of the church requested a vote whether to keep him as pastor. The vote was to keep him, but he resigned saying that he couldn't lead a divided congregation. He was always a person of service and instilled that desire to serve in my sisters and me. He was the kindest, most patient person I have ever known. He was also very strong. I never wanted to disappoint him. Also, he was determined that we receive an education so that we would never have to depend on a man for anything. My mother is probably the most brilliant person I know. She wants to know everything about everything. We were always learning in our family.

How did you choose to specialize in obstetrics and gynecology?
During my surgery rotation in medical school, the surgeon said, "Okay, I'm going to let you make the incision." The minute I did it, I knew I wanted to do surgery. However, I also wanted to take care of women and to educate them about their health. I practiced obstetrics for 20 years and loved it. But the schedule was grueling. One day I was taking my kids for a walk and my phone kept ringing. My son said, "Mommy, when are you going to have time to talk to me?" The next day I told my partners I was switching to gynecology. It's a much easier lifestyle and freed up more time for my family.

Medicine has become big business. You were a founding partner of Women First, an obstetrics and gynecology practice. But you're a reluctant businessperson?
I don't like the business aspect, but I do it because it needs to be done. I'm intrigued by medicine and by why our bodies do what they do. I'm a firm believer that knowledge is power. The more I know, the more I can help other women understand why their bodies and minds are reacting in a certain way, what's causing a medical problem, and what the options are to address the problem.

Do men and women react differently to being ill?
I'll probably get run out of town for saying it, but men are whiny. Women are more able to cope with illness and pain; they pull themselves together. I haven't figured out why we're so much more able to deal with being sick or having things not being perfect!

What has been your major challenge?
Like it is for many women, balancing a career with being a mom. I feel like I haven't done either one as well as I would like.

You don't hesitate to answer when asked about the most defining time in your life.
My dad was diagnosed with cancer on my first day of med school. He died 11 months later at the age of 49. It was brutal. It didn't make me a negative or a depressed person. But it let me understand that happiness doesn't always last, but neither does sadness. It made me stronger and it made me become a much more compassionate doctor because people were very compassionate to me.

As a doctor, do you believe in miracles?
Yes. I've seen them happen. I'm a woman of faith. I pray and meditate every day.

Is there anything that intimidates you?
Mean people.

How do you like to spend your spare time?
Exercising, playing pool, playing the piano, and reading.

What haven't you done that you'd like to do?
Learn to sail.

How do you feel about aging?
I've been through enough that I'm grateful for every day. My 50s are the best time of my life.

Is there something that people would be surprised to know about you?
I officiate at weddings. A dear friend of mine, who is Jewish, was planning to marry a man who is not Jewish. She needed to find someone to perform the marriage because her rabbi wasn't comfortable with a mixed religion ceremony. I went online and became an ordained minister. I performed her ceremony and have done several others.

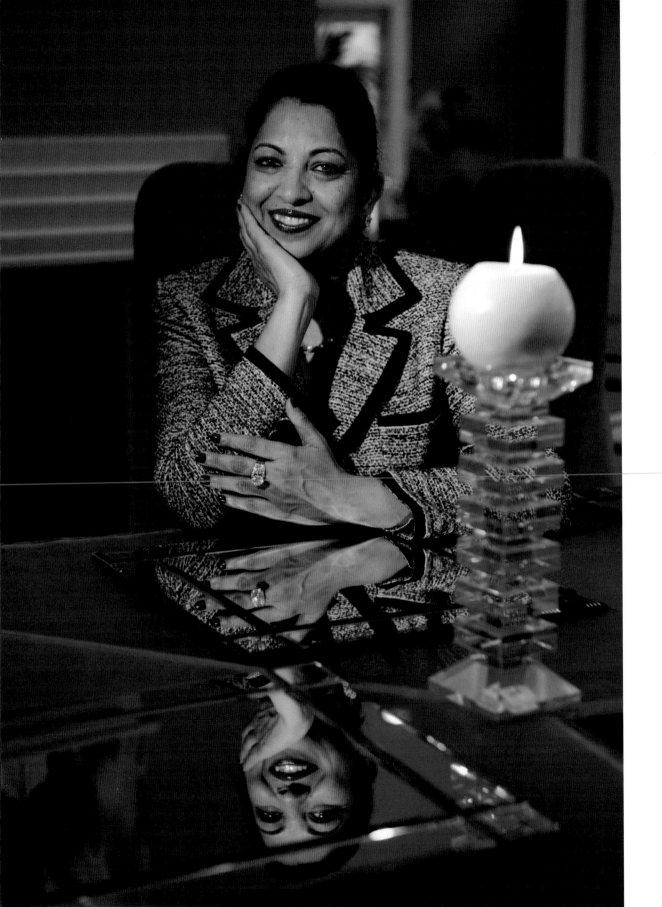

Pushpa Tiwari

You had a fairy tale life growing up in India!

It was wonderful. I'm from Rishikesh, a holy place, and where yoga originated. I had a very, very easy life in which servants did everything for me. All of my friends were also from rich families. We traveled quite a bit because my father wanted me to enjoy everything and to see everything. My dream was to become a doctor, but the nearest medical school was far away. I was very close to my parents, especially to my father. My parents didn't want me to go away to college, so I went to school in my hometown.

Tradition was so important in your family that you agreed to an arranged marriage.

My father began looking for potential husbands for me. He had selected a couple boys for me to consider, but I told him I wanted to meet only one of the boys. I trusted my father 100 percent to find the right person for me. We went to visit Deepak, my future husband, in his city. I was impressed and liked him although he never said anything. Then, when he came to see us, my mother was crazy with getting me ready in the sari and preparing how I'd look. However, I said I wanted to wear simple clothes and no makeup or jewelry. After we were all gathered, Deepak asked my father if he could take me out. But that would have been difficult because everyone in town knew my family. "If you have decided you want to marry her, I'll let her go out with you," said my father.

I liked Deepak because he was very honest. He was from a wealthy doctor's family but told me that he, personally, wasn't making much money as a school principal. But it didn't matter because my family had so much money.

We got married and had two children in India. Deepak wanted to move to the United States but my parents didn't want us to leave India. I was very independent and sold my jewelry for our plane tickets.

You went from a life of luxury in India to a very difficult life in the United States.

Coming to the United States was, at first, a disaster for me. I didn't know how we would survive because of the cultural differences. My husband worked three jobs and I worked in a day-care center. I never told my family in India that we were struggling so much. I had to learn how to do everything, even how to do dishes, mop the floor, and even write a check because I had been so sheltered in India. I learned a lot from the preschool children in the day-care center. I kept a diary and wrote down words they said and then looked them up in a dictionary. But I was so happy because my husband and children and I were together.

Life is very different for you now.

My husband eventually bought a Subway franchise. I worked in the shop seven days a week. We now own 12 Subways and two other restaurants. I run the operations side of our businesses. I never imagined we would be so successful or so happy. My mother, my sister and her husband, and the four of us live in our house. We still lead a very traditional Indian lifestyle.

What has been your major disappointment or regret?

I've been blessed. I have neither.

You've been married 30 years. What's the key to a good marriage?

Understanding and trusting each other. We don't interfere with each other, even in our business.

What's the most important thing you've learned about yourself?

That I have the capability to do a lot of things, and that I learn fast. I'm proud of myself.

Is there anything that intimidates you?

No. Even if we lost everything, I could start over and live nicely. I still have no problem working 12 hours a day. When we came here I had nothing. Someone could take my money but not my intelligence. I could make the money again and so could my husband.

In three words, how would you describe yourself?

Confident, confident, confident.

Is there a major difference between Indian and American women?

If I had stayed in India I would have had to have been a housewife there. I think I have business genes, but I wouldn't have been able to be in business in India because my father would not have permitted it. I'm so glad I had the opportunity to prove myself. But without my husband and kids, and my parents believing in me, I wouldn't have accomplished so much.

What are your favorite indulgences?

Clothes, jewelry and chocolate.

What would you change about yourself if you could?

I'm very emotional and I cry easily. I want to learn how to control my feelings. I'm strong in my professional life, but too emotional in family situations.

Rachel Colvin
Torres

You're a pastry chef. One taste of French pastry and you never looked back!

I was in France planning to teach English. But I was led astray by marzipan and real ganache. I would stare through patisserie windows and spend the afternoon with a carafe of wine and a piece of cake. I understood that I couldn't leave wonderful desserts out of my life. When I hear people say they don't like desserts, I feel sorry for them because they've never had a dessert that knocked their socks off.

One of your bosses was so dreadful she made you cry?

Back in the United States I became an overeducated kitchen worker in hotels and catering companies, but I loved it. My nose was out of the book and I was doing something real. I got a job as assistant pastry chef. You hear about male chefs being mean? My boss was awful and she made me cry. I thought, "She's worked with chefs all over the world and is teaching me what she knows. So who cares if she's mean?"

Now you're the Ooohmami! entrepreneur. What?

I developed Ooohmami!, a blend of all-natural vegetable and nutritional ingredients that evoke the fifth taste called umami. Ooohmami! uses synergistic combinations of organic shiitake mushrooms, kelp, nutritional yeast, and organic tomatoes to bring out this flavor without the use of any animal or synthetic products.

You have said you'd rather starve than eat cake from a mix. Really?

Never in my life would I fix a cake from a box. Tastes like chemicals and not at all worth the calories. I'm also obsessed with lemons and hate anything with fake lemon. It tastes like furniture polish.

One night you went dancing and met a man. From then on…

My brother and I had been taking salsa lessons. One night I wanted to go to a Latin club but he was busy. I went by myself. There was only one other person there. He was a soldier just back from Iraq. I was dancing in five-inch stilettos. He came up to my chest but wasn't intimidated at all. His confidence was very attractive to me. He led me around the dance floor even though I was like a tree. We were inseparable from that night on. Now we're married with a wonderful little girl.

Your husband is deployed yet again to a war zone. How do you cope with his absence and the constant worrying about him?

I don't watch CNN and I stay very busy teaching yoga and laughing at my hilarious little girl, Isvara. It's very helpful that I'm 42 and not 22. I have lived on my own for a long time, and am consequently very independent, so that helps.

You suffered a brain tumor not long after your daughter was born. How did that change your life?

My perspective on everything changed. Eight percent of people with subdural hematomas (brain bleeds) don't survive, and I had two this past year, ending in a not so cute scar from the craniotomy and 100 stitches down my head. I wrote my daughter a book about everything I needed to tell her, and am working on a self-defense/yoga workshop for teenage girls. The hematoma could come back at any time. My skull is very thick (feel free to make thick skull jokes. I do.) and my brain doesn't have much room to move around, so I have to very careful—no upside down yoga or running for me. But I am so grateful to be alive. It just lit a fire under me to go after everything I want in life.

With which person of note would you most like to spend the day?

Clint Eastwood. He's the perfect combination of a tough guy, brilliant musician, and director. I'd also like to spend another day with Nelson Mandela.

What would you change about yourself if you could?

I'd improve my listening and patience. My enthusiasm might be appealing, but I never shut up.

What's in your future?

We're going to move to Ecuador after my husband gets out of the service. I'm going to teach yoga, bake, and paint. And I'm going to have a huge garden. It's going to be Eden, absolutely blissful.

Carol Rawert Trainer

You were arrested during a high-profile antiwar protest at Abbey Road on the River.

I stood up for my rights that day but found out I didn't have any rights. I'm still in shock. I had been at the festival for five hours holding a small sign that said End the War. Three men who were drinking told me to go home because the crowd wanted to have fun. I responded by saying that I was going to stay there to remind everyone that people in Iraq weren't having fun. I forced myself about three inches from the mayor's eyes. He glared at me like I had two holes in my head. I was arrested. That was one of the hardest times of my life. I'll never forget it and it's why I could never vote for a ticket with Abramson on it. I blame a lot of my arrest on him.

When did you become involved in the antiwar movement?

Before the War in Afghanistan, around 2000. It was evident to a lot of us that the war was based on lies, and the lies kept changing. It was scary to think we'd go into a war after the Vietnam War. I thought, "Here we go again." My husband and I got involved with the Louisville Peace Action Committee with Sister Miriam Corcoran. We held monthly vigils for years.

Today's antiwar movement seems to lack energy and definition

The commitment isn't there. You just see a bunch of old people. Without the draft and without television showing the flag-draped coffins coming back home, it's easy to forget there's a war going on. The media and the White House keep it sanitized.

You, the activist, were also in the Air Force. Where was your heart?

I listened to JFK's speech about ask not what your country can do for you, ask what you can do for your country. I was idealistic and believed the government propaganda about the Vietnam War. Now I don't believe a thing the government says.

Are you still a feminist?

Somewhat. I'm not a radical feminist. I think some feminists are a little extreme. We have a long way to go. I'm 65 and not out pounding the pavement. Other women will have to worry about it.

Candidate Obama talked about hope and change. Is President Obama talking a different message?

A lot of people, including me, hoped things would change when Obama got in but they didn't. He said he would end the war by a certain date and would close Guantanamo. But when he got in office he became privy to things he hadn't known before. Maybe he was too young and inexperienced for the job. Plus, he probably realized he had to save his own job. I worked on Obama's campaign but after he didn't do anything when he got in, my husband and I switched from Democrats to Independent as a protest. I don't know if I'd vote for him again.

Do you support civil disobedience?

Yes, as long as people aren't hurt.

Do you see an end to the wars in which we are involved?

Not unless we have a war tax and a draft.

Is war ever justified?

I'm not a pacifist although I think the world, for the most part, could do away with war by talking and supporting each other more. During World War II we had to do something to stop Hitler. I have a close connection to that war because my third cousin in Germany was rounded up by the Nazis who threatened to kill him if he didn't join them.

You lived through a parent's worst nightmare.

My son died when he was 13 years old. How did I get through it? After five bereavement days, I went back to work as a software support supervisor. Work gave me something else to think about.

Do you think you've "found" yourself?

Definitely. I started feeling that way at 29 years old. I knew then what I wanted and who I was. I never thought I'd be an antiwar activist because I was in the Air Force and my husband was a major in the Air Force. Now the antiwar movement has taken over our lives. But I had a mini stroke in December. Since then I've taken a close look at my life. I can't keep going full steam in the movement. I'm trying to step back a little but still do what I need to do. I don't know how people can sit by and do nothing. I couldn't live with myself if I did that.

Teresa Pasquini
Wallace

You're a "roller derby girl." There must be a story behind that!

When I was six years old, I told my mother I wanted to be a dancer or a roller girl. I thought it would be so neat to play roller derby and be on television. I became a rink rat girl, someone who was always hanging around the skating rink. Later on, I had a friend who joined the Derby City Roller Girls. I watched her play and the next day I showed up for practice and never quit.

And you found love on the rink?

My husband and I met when he went to a bout with some friends. He was smitten by my skating. He's a good sport when I play and get kind of rough with him. He's become one of the husbands known as derby widowers.

Roller derby is a very hot sport. The Derby City Roller Girls are making quite a name for themselves, aren't they?

There are more than 500 roller derby leagues in the world. Ours is the only team in Louisville, so we play regionally and nationally. We're part of the Women's Flat Track Derby Association. It's like the NBA for roller derby.

Why are you so passionate about roller derby?

It's super-competitive. It's also very much a team sport, but we're all so different. You really have to put your heart and soul into it. We feel like we're part of something big because of the roller derby resurgence. It's not like the old wrestling kind of sport. There's a book of rules and we have to take a yearly test. It's all about getting better and better, and learning strategy.

You even have your own roller derby name.

Yes, it's Lil' Bo Peep and my number is 4H. I chose it because it goes with the whole country thing that I love. I'm baaaad to the bone. My bloomers used to say, "Ewe can't touch this."

Are people surprised to learn you play roller derby?

For sure. It cracks me up. I suppose they're especially surprised because I'm also in the professional world. I'm a sales rep for a home healthcare company. I call on physicians' offices and assisted-living centers. I promote healing through occupational and physical therapy. It's kind of funny that I leave that and then try to hurt people on the rink!

And do you get hurt?

I have developed some knee problems and shin splints. Getting hurt is part of the sport.

So you must be pretty fearless.

In a way, I suppose. I used to like rock climbing and mountain biking. But when I think of fear I think of swimming.

What's really important in your life other than roller derby?

I come from a large, traditional family. I love visiting my extended family in Italy. They shower me with affection. I am so close to them and don't feel like we live halfway around the world. My 95-year-old grandmother lives here in Louisville and is my best friend. We have a blast. She really tells it how it is. She's strong, full of stories, and very witty. I think the key to staying healthy and being happy as you age is having a sense of humor.

You seem very attached to your roots in Italy.

I have dual citizenship and can vote there. I'd love to live there.

What's your biggest regret?

That I didn't travel more when I was younger. I've been on my own since I was 17. As the oldest of four kids, I was kind of the Little Mamma even though my own mother did a great job. I never borrowed a penny from anyone because I was always very self-sufficient. I've always been so responsible that I've turned down lots of opportunities for fun.

Do you think you've found yourself?

I'm comfortable with who I am. I don't get my feelings hurt like I used to because I'm aware of myself. But I'm not sure I've truly found myself. I'm still trying to figure it out.

What haven't you done that you'd like to do?

Have kids, but I'm scared to death. Besides my husband, Lucky, our Boston terrier, is the love of my life now. He's my everything.

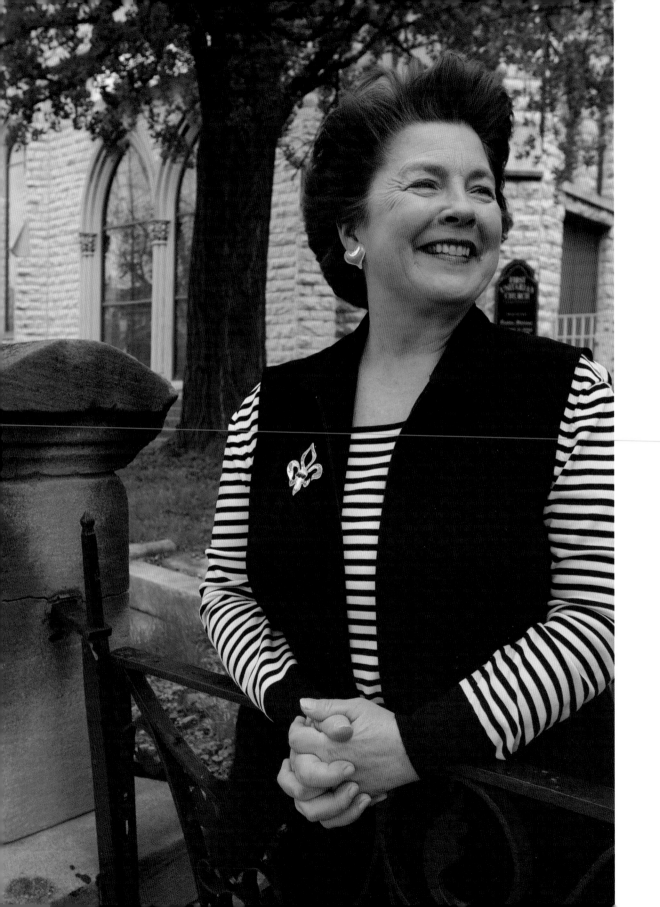

Marsha Weinstein

You're a staunch feminist. The word has different meanings for different people. What does it mean to you?

To me it means women and men are equal. They shouldn't have obstacles put in their way. The real core of the problem rests with religion and many religious cultures. I'm not into the theory of feminism. I'm into activism.

Are you optimistic about the future?

Our democracy is a mess because of corporations and special interest groups. I'm optimistic because we're in the last grasp of male dominance. The white male will be a minority in a few decades, so white power brokers won't control everything as they have in the past. I'm also hopeful about the future because of technology. Major media don't control all of the information anymore. It makes for more of a level playing field. I use social media to create social change and to reach out to people, especially young people.

You are past president of the Louisville League of Women Voters, and were chair of the nominating committee for the League of Women Voters in the United States. The League has been criticized as left leaning. How do you respond to that?

Yes, we have been criticized of that. But I think a highly educated person who understands the issues will naturally lean to liberalism.

Don't you think there will be many people who will be shocked at such an assertion and will strongly disagree with that statement?

I believe in the "evolution of consciousness," which means when people are open to new ideas and respect others they are able to move out of "darkness" and into the "light."

You've said that one of your proudest accomplishments was persuading Governor Jones to grant clemency to 10 women who killed or attempted to kill their abusers.

Much of their voice had been expressed through the creation of quilts because they couldn't publicly talk about their past. They said they didn't think the public cared about domestic violence. I suggested they make a quilt as art therapy to reflect what they had lived through and felt. When the governor saw the quilt, he started to cry and said, "Marsha, we have to get these women out of prison." It was a very powerful way to learn how art can speak for and to people. Gov. Fletcher later gave them complete pardons and also let another group out of prison.

In a few words, how would you describe yourself?

Passionate. Determined. Persistent. If someone tells me "no" I just think of it as a delayed "yes."

What's the best decision you've made?

Marrying my husband. He's a feminist and has supported me in all my endeavors and has made it possible for me to follow my dreams. You have to kiss a lot of toads before you find your prince. I kissed some toads, and then I found my prince.

What's your best advice to girls?

Find your dream. Follow your heart. Everyone has a gift. Do what you believe in and stand by your beliefs. People want to silence girls. You'll know you're doing something good when people get upset with you.

What motivates and inspires you?

Girls give me energy, which motivates me, and reading women's history inspires me.

What has been the biggest challenge in your life?

The biggest challenge of my life was when I first became a mother—however, my children have been my greatest blessing!

And your major disappointment?

My only disappointment has been when I have not lived up to the standards I set for myself.

Other than the people in your life, what couldn't you live without?

I could not live without nature—trees, flowers, mountains, water, animals, rainbows.

What's the most important thing you've learned about yourself?

To trust my instincts.

What has been the most defining moment in your life?

When I realized that I was never taught women's history in school and the importance of women's contributions to the development of our nation and world. The accomplishments of our foremothers inspire me to also make contributions.

What haven't you done that you would like to do?

Write my life's story.

Ann Wells

You now head up one of Louisville's most respected banks. But your background is in electrical engineering. There must be a story behind that!

Ever since I was a little girl, I wanted to be an engineer like my dad. In school my favorite subjects were math and science so it seemed like a natural progression to study engineering in college.

As chairman and CEO of Commonwealth Bank & Trust Company, you're one of the city's most powerful and influential people. With that power and influence comes a great deal of responsibility. How do you view your role in the community?

I don't see myself as powerful and influential. But if people think I'm powerful and influential and that helps accomplish the goal, then that's fine. I feel everyone has a responsibility to improve the community they live in. I take that responsibility very seriously on both a personal and professional level.

Aren't the top echelons of banking still a man's world? Have you encountered, or do you still encounter, differential treatment because you're a woman?

You have to understand that as an engineer in the late '60s and '70s, I saw more than my share of discrimination against women in the workplace. I wish it were a gender-blind world. Fortunately, I have not experienced the same problems in banking.

Being such a visible person in the community, do you always have to be on guard about what you say and do, even when you're away from the bank or at an official function?

My mother always taught my sister and me to conduct ourselves as ladies. I know Mom is still watching over me so I had better behave!

What has been the biggest challenge in your life?

I think I have had a pretty charmed life. Good parents, a great husband, and wonderful children. I would rather look forward to whatever the next challenges or opportunities might be ahead.

What has been the most significant accomplishment of your life?

My four children—Laura, Liz, Lee, and Eleanor!

Other than the people in your life, what couldn't you live without?

My quiet time to read, do needlepoint, and do Sudoku.

What's the biggest risk you have ever taken?

Marrying my husband six months after meeting him on a blind date. It was a good risk as we just celebrated our 40th wedding anniversary.

Is there anything that intimidates you?

I have an absolutely controlling fear of snakes. I don't garden because I might meet a snake. When I was a little girl, a snake crawled over my foot. I may have made some progress when my son Lee made me touch a boa constrictor at the zoo. I closed my eyes and touched it quickly. And, I might have been confronting my fear when before my 50th birthday I wanted to do everything I hadn't done before and went white-water rafting in Colorado. We slept on a cot on the ground and were told not to roll out our bed roll until we were ready to go to sleep because something might get into it.

In three or four words how would you describe yourself?

Capable, persistent, a doer, a caring person.

What has been the most defining moment in your life?

I take whatever comes and accept whatever challenges come along. I believe in that adage, God won't send you anything you can't handle.

What haven't you done that you would like to do?

Learn to pilot a plane.

What's the best decision you have ever made?

Marrying Darrell Wells.

What do you like best about yourself?

My independent spirit.

And least?

I don't think that way. I try to stay focused on the positive.

What's your biggest regret?

Not slowing down to savor the special moments.

What would people be surprised to know about you?

That I am shy.

Is there anything you would change about yourself if you could?

I would love to be thin! And also to have more patience.

Cia White

You're an English teacher and you teach creative writing. When will we be able to read your own story?

The sad story is that I have a closet full of manuscripts. I have had a pretty varied adventure of a life. My father was a close friend of Lyndon Johnson. My parents' lives changed radically because of their friendship with him. The sad fact is that their involvement in politics broke both of them personally. I witnessed my father break down at about the same rate as Johnson did. It's hard for me to discuss it in the terms that might attract interest in a book. I was an antiwar hippie and went to school at Stanford. My 20s and 30s were about experiencing a different life than the one I was meant to have by my upper middle-class education in Washington, D.C. My husband of many years and I traveled across the country for a year and a half going to roadhouses and honky tonks with the intention of writing a book about honky tonks. But I settled down and lived on a farm with him for 14 years. I got to see the sort of last gasp of a healthy, small tobacco farm growing culture.

You lived in a tree. That deserves an explanation.

It was a redwood tree, a burned-out 20-foot high sequoia stump on the land belonging to the author Ken Kesey. The tree was the size of a small living room. It was great. Luckily, I had friends who were house sitting at the Keseys' where there was a hot tub and a bathroom.

What's the biggest risk you have ever taken?

To come out when I was in my 40s. It was very, very difficult. As Anne, my partner, says, those are the war criminal years. When you come out, you're responding to a lifelong series of attractions and secrets and shames and guilt. It isn't just in that moment or that decade that it happens. I had a miserable divorce and my kids suffered that. The transition was so abrupt; it was hard for them and for me. It was terrifying. Also, it was disappointing to learn that some people I thought were friends were not my friends at all. However, my dearest friends had my back. Coming out was the most defining time of my life in metaphorical ways as well as the literal way. It was the moment my real life could begin. I feel lucky to have survived and come out on the other side.

Do you have advice for other women who are thinking of coming out?

The prospect of concealing your affectional word is supposed to be life for the rest of your life rather than taking the risk of claiming it seems a terrible choice.

Other than the people in your life, what couldn't you live without?

Books.

Do you ever read trashy novels?

No. I'm a total book snob. But I acknowledge that there are different ways and reasons to read books.

What would people be surprised to know about you?

That I'm very, very shy.

How do you measure success?

By a passionate commitment to seeing things through, and having a sense of humor and a sense of proportion.

What's the most important thing you have learned about yourself?

That I second guess myself too often. Having too much hesitation to go with my instinctive feelings about something is not a good path. And I have learned I have to constantly temper my inclination to approach things intellectually rather than through relationships.

How would you finish the sentence, "I wish women would…

fight harder for equality of opportunity." By that I mean fighting for changes in family structure and child raising. In ways, it is still unbelievably hard to be female in the United States.

How do you feel about aging?

I've been lucky that, at this point, I haven't felt a lot of physical changes. But at times I feel kind of curmudgeonly. I don't like the world weariness that comes from aging. There's so much of vital interest to younger people that is of absolutely no interest to me. I watched my mother get more and more negative about contemporary phenomena. At that time I thought maybe that was a necessary psychological adjustment so that you don't regret too much leaving this world.

What would you change about yourself if you could?

To be 25 years younger. I'd like to do it all again.